Parfait Press
An imprint of the Baker & Taylor Publishing Group
10350 Barnes Canyon Road, San Diego, CA 92121

Library of Congress Cataloging-in-Publication Data

You wouldn't want to sail the seas! / Peter Cook ... [et al.].
   p. cm.
 Audience: Age 8.
 ISBN-13: 978-1-60710-472-8
 ISBN-10: 1-60710-472-5
1. Seafaring life--Juvenile literature. 2. Ocean travel--Juvenile literature. 3. Ships--History--Juvenile literature. 4. Shipwreck survival--Juvenile literature. I. Cook, Peter, 1946 May 13-
 G540.Y68 2012
 910.4'5--dc23
            2012000671

Manufactured, printed, and assembled in Guangdong, China.
1 2 3 4 5 15 14 13 12

You Wouldn't Want to Sail the Seas!

Written by
Peter Cook
John Malam
Jim Pipe
David Stewart

Illustrated by
David Antram
Kevin Whelan

Created and designed by
David Salariya

parfait press

San Diego, California

Contents

Those in Peril on the Sea

"Worse things happen at sea," says an old proverb. This expression is meant to make you feel better when things aren't going too well. But suppose you really *are* at sea—what's the worst that could happen?

The true stories in this book describe some of the most arduous voyages that anyone has endured. Over hundreds of years, sailors and passengers have risked storms, cannonballs, leaky ships, starvation, disease, piracy. Why? Some sailed to make war on their enemies, while others went in search of a better life in a new land. Some went to sea to earn their living, and others sailed just for pleasure.

Unsinkable?

In 1907, Captain Edward Smith proudly stated: "I cannot imagine any condition which would cause a ship to founder [sink]. . . . Modern shipbuilding has gone beyond that." Five years later, Captain Smith was in charge of the *Titanic*, a fine modern ship that was regarded as the safest vessel afloat. It was carefully designed to survive any kind of accident—except for the one that actually happened to it…

Today, ships are safer than they have ever been. They have radar, sonar, radio, and all kinds of safety devices; they can call for help at any time from professional emergency services. Disasters like those described in this book rarely happen today—but still the sea is a force of nature that can never be under our control.

Collectible scrimshaws

You Wouldn't Want to Sail in the Spanish Armada!

Introduction

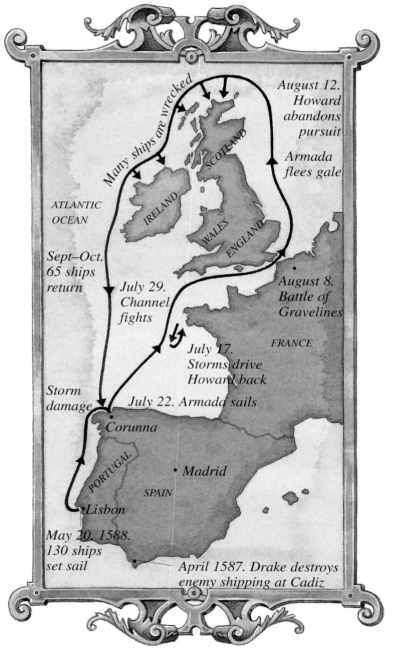

August 12. Howard abandons pursuit

Armada flees gale

Many ships are wrecked

SCOTLAND

IRELAND

WALES

ENGLAND

ATLANTIC OCEAN

Sept–Oct. 65 ships return

July 29. Channel fights

August 8. Battle of Gravelines

July 17. Storms drive Howard back

FRANCE

Storm damage

July 22. Armada sails

Corunna

PORTUGAL

Madrid

SPAIN

Lisbon

May 20, 1588. 130 ships set sail

April 1587. Drake destroys enemy shipping at Cadiz

Route taken by the Spanish Armada, 1587—1588

It is May in the year 1588, and you are about to set off on a daring voyage. You are a sailor in the service of King Philip II of Spain, and your country is about to send *la felicissima armada* (Spanish for "the most fortunate fleet") to invade England, your enemy. The Armada's mission is to land soldiers on English soil. Spain's brave fighting men will conquer that annoying little country and then King Philip will be the ruler of England as well as Spain. He wants to change England's religion and to return the country to being a Roman Catholic nation. The invasion will be difficult and as you plot your course, you will soon know if you would—or wouldn't—want to be in the Spanish Armada.

Enemies – Spain Against England

Why 16th-Century Spain Doesn't Like England

RELIGION. In 1533, Henry VIII of England turned his back on the Pope. King Philip of Spain wants to make England turn back to the Roman Catholic Church.

Spain and England have been enemies for years—ever since King Henry VIII broke away from the Catholic Church and invented the Church of England. Catholics were angry. When Henry VIII's daughter, Elizabeth, became queen and head of the Church of England, King Philip II of Spain was furious. Later, when Elizabeth executed Mary Stuart, he decided to teach the English a lesson. He planned to invade England, but the English found out and on April 19, 1587, Sir Francis Drake destroyed the Spanish ships in Cadiz Harbor. He said he'd "singed the king of Spain's beard"—what an insult!

VENGEANCE. In 1587, Elizabeth I ordered the execution of Mary Stuart, Queen of Scots. Mary was a Roman Catholic who supported Spain. King Philip wants to punish England for her death.

RIVALRY. Spain and England both want to control trade with the "New World"—the Americas. English privateers attack Spain's ships bringing treasure from the Americas and King Philip wants to stop them.

Who's Who?

ELIZABETH I became queen of England in 1558.

PHILIP II, king of Spain since 1556.

SIR FRANCIS DRAKE, an English privateer.

April 19, 1587

Handy Hint
Learn to swim. If you end up in the water, you'll have to swim to safety or drown.

Spanish ships destroyed in Cadiz Harbor

Get Ready! The Armada Gathers

After Sir Francis Drake's attack on the ships at Cadiz, your king orders the Marquis of Santa Cruz to assemble a fleet of ships. He will teach those English a lesson! This fleet is the king's Great Armada, which will take an invasion force to England. The king wants the Armada to sail as soon as Santa Cruz has the ships and troops ready—but Santa Cruz has a different idea. The king wanted a surprise attack, but Santa Cruz didn't want the ships to sail in the rough winter seas. Portugal is under Spanish control at this time, so Santa Cruz gathers the fleet off the coast of Lisbon, Portugal, and waits for better weather.

King Philip in Madrid

Why hasn't my Armada sailed?

Life as a Spanish Sailor

BAD FOOD. There are maggots in everything, and if you don't eat your food, they will.

SOGGY BED. When it rains, water drips through gaps in the ship's timbers. It drips on you while you're asleep.

NOISE, SMELLS, AND DIRT. It's cramped and gloomy belowdecks, and it's always noisy, smelly, and very dirty.

December 1587

Marquis of Santa Cruz in Lisbon

His Armada can wait till spring!

Handy Hint
Cheer up, life's not that bad! Drink your daily wine ration—it'll make you feel tipsy and you'll soon forget your troubles.

DISEASE. The bad food and drinking water, and the dirty ship, are the perfect conditions for diseases to spread. Check your body for spots and lice.

SICK SANTA. In January 1588, the Marquis of Santa Cruz lies dying of typhus.

11

Cast Off! The Armada Sails

Santa Cruz dies in February 1588. Your new leader is the Duke of Medina Sidonia, a rich landowner. Would you have chosen him? He's got no experience of ships or warfare at sea, and he's told the king he gets seasick! You hope this is not a bad omen. After a long wait, you finally sail for England. Between May 28 and 30, 1588, the Invincible Armada (as you call it) of about 130 ships sails from Lisbon.

Armada Who's Who?

Commander Don Alonso Pérez de Guzmán, Duke of Medina Sidonia.

SOLDIERS and SAILORS. About 20,000 soldiers are packed onto the ships. They will fight in England. The ships are crewed by 8,000 sailors, including you.

The Fleet

FOUR GALLEYS and FOUR GALLEASSES. Slaves row these large, armed ships when there is no wind in their sails.

ARMED MERCHANTMEN. Forty of these ships carry all the food and equipment—weapons, horses, mules, tents, and other supplies.

SERVICE SHIPS. Thirty-four small, fast ships take messages between ships and from ship to shore. They will also sail ahead as scouts.

May 1588

PRIESTS AND SURGEONS. About 180 priests sail with you. They plan to convert England back to Roman Catholicism. In the hospital ship are about 85 surgeons and doctors—in case of casualties.

Handy Hint

Pray for victory. On April 25, go to Lisbon Cathedral, where the Archbishop of Lisbon will bless the Armada before it sails.

SLAVES. About 2,000 slaves row the Armada's galleys.

FIREPOWER. Altogether the ships of the Armada have 2,477 guns of various sizes.

TWENTY WAR GALLEONS. These large, heavy ships have two or three decks and three masts. Each one is armed with about 40 guns and carries about 400 men.

13

Storm! The Armada Is Forced to Wait

The Armada sails north to the Spanish port of Corunna, arriving on June 19, 1588. The ships are loaded with supplies. During the night a storm blows in from the Atlantic, scattering the fleet, which cannot sail on until the storm is over. You discover that the Armada is bound for the port of Calais in the Spanish Netherlands (modern France), where 21,000 Spanish troops will board the ships. They are men of the Duke of Parma's army and the Armada will take them across the English Channel to invade England. Unknown to you, the English know the plan and have sent ships to attack the Armada.

DUKE OF PARMA. He is King Philip's governor-general in the Spanish Netherlands.

LORD HOWARD OF EFFINGHAM. He leads the English fleet and must stop the Armada.

SEASICKNESS. It's the first time most of the Spanish soldiers have been to sea.

Saved by the Storm

THE ENGLISH ARE COMING. Queen Elizabeth has sent about 100 ships to seek out and destroy the Armada before it reaches England.

GETTING CLOSE. The English hope to attack you while you're in port at Corunna.

BLOWN HOME. The storm that scattered your ships forces Elizabeth's fleet back to England. The storm has saved you.

Seen by an English Ship!

You think the weather is on your side. Toward the end of July, a strong wind blows the Armada from Corunna close to the English coast (the same wind that blew the English ships away from Spain). Your ships gather off the Isles of Scilly before sailing along the English Channel. But the English are expecting you. On July 29, Thomas Fleming, on a little ship called the *Golden Hinde*, spots the Armada. He sails back to Plymouth, on the south coast of England, with the bad news.

July 29, 1588

The English Reaction

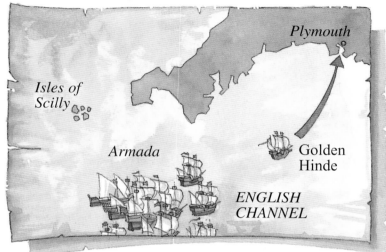

Plymouth

Isles of Scilly

Armada

Golden Hinde

ENGLISH CHANNEL

Handy Hint

Don't let the English take you by surprise. Get your ship's cannons ready for action.

RACE HOME. The *Golden Hinde* takes a day to sail to Plymouth 80 miles away.

BOWLS. Fleming tells Drake the Armada is coming, but he is lawn bowling! He replies, "Time to finish the game and then beat the Spaniards!"

BEACONS. The English light beacons across the country. These fires spread the news that the Armada is on its way to attack England.

ACTION PLAN. The English act fast. Sea captains check their charts, and within hours, their ships leave Plymouth, ready to face the Armada.

BIG GUNS. *Triumph*, an English ship, has 42 guns and is England's biggest ship. On board are 500 sailors, gunners, and soldiers.

17

The Chase Along the Channel

The Armada sails in a crescent formation along the English Channel. Heavily armed galleons lead so they can be first to fight the English. As you sail to Calais, to pick up the Duke of Parma's 20,000 soldiers, English ships approach you from behind. Drake leads one English squadron. The English fire their cannons and some of your ships are damaged. But the worst damage is caused when the *San Salvador* suddenly explodes. A powder barrel has ignited, and the galleon burns up.

Events in the Channel

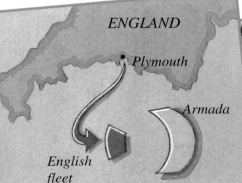

JULY 30. The Armada is sighted off the coast of Cornwall. The fleet is sailing east along the English Channel.

JULY 31. The English fleet, of about 50 ships, leaves Plymouth and chases the Armada along the Channel.

AUGUST 1. Messages of instruction go to each Armada ship. The Duke of Parma is told to move his men to Calais and wait for them to be collected.

July 31, 1588

The San Salvador explodes

Handy Hint

Prepare for close-range fighting. Climb the rigging with missiles to throw at an English ship.

BOOM!

England here I come!

AUGUST 1. The English seize the wreck of the *San Salvador* and tow it back to England.

AUGUST 2–3. Your ships get close to the enemy. You try to board, but their smaller, faster ships out-maneuver you. They blast you with their cannons.

Boom! Fire the Cannons

Firing Your Cannon

As you approach the Isle of Wight, you are attacked by the English fleet. You must fire back. Your cannon is a culverin—a gun that's 11 feet long and weighs a deck-smashing 4,500 pounds. It can throw a 5-inch, 17-pound iron cannonball a distance of about 400 yards. Unfortunately, the English have more big guns and better gunners than you. You're soon getting low on gunpowder and ammunition. Things are starting to look bad for you and the Armada.

INSERT CHARGE. Collect a charge of gunpowder packed in a canvas cylinder from belowdecks. Put it down the muzzle of the cannon.

RAM IT IN. Push the charge down to the breech (bottom) of the cannon.

WAD THE CHARGE. Stuff some wadding made from shredded rope down the barrel.

LOAD A SHOT. Roll the cannonball (the shot) down the barrel.

WAD THE SHOT. Pack more wadding into the barrel.

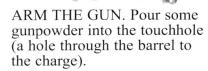

ARM THE GUN. Pour some gunpowder into the touchhole (a hole through the barrel to the charge).

TAKE AIM. Move the cannon so it points at an enemy ship.

FIRE! Put a burning match in the touchhole and stand back!

BOOM

Fireships! The English Try to Burn the Armada

On August 6, the Armada reaches Calais. Your ships lie ready to pick up the Duke of Parma's army. But the English have a clever plan. Their ships are upwind of yours, which means the wind is blowing from them to you. This means the Armada is open to attack by English fireships loaded with gunpowder and combustible material. The English know you're waiting to collect an army, so that night they send blazing fireships toward you. As these floating bombs approach, everyone panics. Anchor cables are cut and the Armada scatters. In the darkness, many ships collide with each other.

The English Fireships

EIGHT SHIPS. One of the eight 220-ton fireships is the *Thomas Drake*—owned by Sir Francis Drake himself.

Handy Hint

Tie a barrel to your anchor cable. It will float, so you'll know where your anchor is when daybreak comes.

LOADED! The English fireships' cannons are armed, so they'll explode in the fire and do even more damage to your ships.

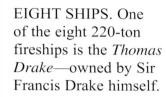

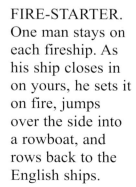

TAR, PITCH, AND HEMP. Tar, pitch, old hemp ropes, anything that will burn is loaded onto the ships so they'll burn well.

FIRE-STARTER. One man stays on each fireship. As his ship closes in on yours, he sets it on fire, jumps over the side into a rowboat, and rows back to the English ships.

23

Shot At! The Battle of Gravelines

As dawn breaks on August 8, you see that the Armada's ships are scattered. Orders come to regroup around Medina Sidonia's flagship, the *San Martín*. As you sail into position, the *San Martín* and three other galleons attack the English fleet off Gravelines, close to Calais. It is a fierce fight. A heavy rain squall blows in during the afternoon and one by one your ships are blown into the North Sea. There is no sign of the Duke of Parma's army and you have no more ammunition. You cannot invade England now.

Battle Tactics

CLOSE RANGE. Your ammunition is low, so only fire close to the English ships—you're more likely to hit them.

GUNS. You're close enough to shoot at the English with your musket—but they'll be shooting at you too.

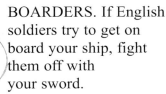

BOARDERS. If English soldiers try to get on board your ship, fight them off with your sword.

STOP LEAKS. If your ship springs a leak, patch it with sheets of lead. Be quick or the ship will sink.

Blown Around Britain

t's a relief to be going home, but you can't return the way you came. The wind is against you and the English are behind you. You'll have to take the long route back, which means sailing north up the east coast of England, right around Scotland, and then south down the west coast of Ireland. The weather is on the side of the English and for the first few days they chase you up the North Sea.

Misery On Board Ship

FOOD SHORTAGES. Food and water have almost run out. You hope they'll last until you reach Spain.

OVERBOARD. The animals that came with you are thrown overboard. They're not needed now, and they'll only drink precious water.

LAST SHOT. You hope the English don't engage you in any more battles— soon there'll be no more ammunition on board your ship.

August 10-11, 1588

Handy Hint

Keep your spirits up. Sing, dance, tell a joke—anything to keep you from feeling as gloomy as your shipmates.

DISEASE. Men are becoming sick. You hope you don't catch whatever it is they've got.

LEAKY SHIP. Your ship's been hit and water is seeping through the hull. You hope you don't sink.

HOMESICK. Morale is low. Everyone just wants to get home quickly and safely.

27

Wrecked! The Ship Is Lost

It Could Have Been You

The English give up the chase on August 12 because they know the Armada's defeated. But you're still in danger. As the remains of the Armada sails around the coasts of Scotland and Ireland, the wind blows the ships toward shore, where many are smashed on the rocks. This happens to your ship off the coast of Ireland.

MASSACRED. Many of your fellow shipmates are washed up on the Irish beaches. Some are caught, stripped, and shot.

HANGED. Those not shot are hanged.

DROWNED. Thousands drown, becoming fish food.

Grab my hand!

28

Your shipmates who make it ashore are treated roughly by the locals. But you're rescued by another ship—you may yet live to see Spain again!

Handy Hint

Ireland, like Spain, is a Catholic country. If you do find yourself there, ask a priest for food and shelter.

Wreckers at Work

The locals steal anything they can get their hands on, from dead mens' clothes to the timbers of wrecked ships. This is called "wrecking."

29

Home!
Back to Spain

O f the 130 ships that left Lisbon in May, only about 65 limp back to Corunna. You reach there on September 21, but it will be many days before the other ships arrive. After weeks at sea you are war-weary and weak. But at least you've survived to tell your sorry tale. About 11,000 of your countrymen were not so lucky—they died in the ill-fated mission to conquer England.

I'm never going to sea again!

What Happened Next?

KING PHILIP II. He built a new navy for another attack on England.

THE SECOND ARMADA. In 1589, the new fleet sailed for England. But a storm wrecked it and Philip's plans.

QUEEN ELIZABETH I. She was now more famous than ever.

September 21, 1588

Handy Hint

Settle down and enjoy life. One day you'll tell your grandchildren you survived King Philip's "invincible Armada"!

FRANCIS DRAKE. In 1589 he led 150 ships in an attempt to help Portugal get its freedom from Spain. He failed.

LORD HOWARD. In 1591 he attacked a large Spanish treasure fleet, but was beaten. He died on board the Spanish flagship.

PEACE AT LAST. It was not until 1604, during the reign of King James I, that Spain and England made peace.

You Wouldn't Want to Sail on the Mayflower!

Introduction

our name is Priscilla Mullins and you are about to embark on one of the most famous journeys in American history—the voyage of the *Mayflower*. The year is 1620 and you are traveling with your parents and brother to escape religious persecution in England and to make a better life in the New World. Carrying 102 passengers—known as Pilgrims—the *Mayflower* is headed for the colony of Virginia on the east coast of America. But the ship is blown off course and eventually lands on the coast of present-day Massachusetts, where a colony is established at Plymouth.

But this is in the future. First you must endure the hardships of the voyage: the cramped conditions, lack of privacy, poor food, and the winter storms of the Atlantic Ocean. It is a journey that will eventually leave you an orphan and there are many times when you wish that you had avoided sailing on the *Mayflower*—a trip that took entirely too long!

33

The Pilgrims

Your father was one of a small group of English Puritans that later became known as the Pilgrims. In the early 1600s a group of "Separatists" had broken away from the Church of England. They wanted to lead a simple life, based on the teachings of the Bible. In 1608 a group of Pilgrims led by William Brewster emigrated to Holland to escape religious persecution. They settled in Leiden, but were still unhappy with the restrictions on their civil rights. About half of the congregation voted to emigrate to America, deciding to settle in the colony of Virginia.

Priscilla Mullins (you)

William (father)

Alice (mother)

Robert Carter (servant)

Joseph (brother)

YOU WERE BORN in about 1602 in Dorking, a small village in the county of Surrey in southern England. Along with your family and a servant, you travel to the port of Southampton on the south coast of England. From there you will begin your voyage to the New World.

WILLIAM BREWSTER is the "ruling elder" of the Leiden Separatists and the Pilgrims' religious leader.

THE PILGRIM FATHERS is the name given to the colonists who will sail aboard the *Mayflower*.

THE LONDON VIRGINIA COMPANY holds the charter for Virginia and authorizes the Pilgrims' proposed new settlement.

Freedom of Worship

THE PEOPLE WHO JOIN the *Mayflower* are known as "Separatists" because they don't follow the religious practices of the Church of England. They want a church where the minister and the congregation are more equal: where the clergy has no direct political power and where there is no need for clerical robes, altars, or kneeling for prayers.

Handy Hint

Don't become a Pilgrim—you could be persecuted for your beliefs!

Bless our congregation, Lord.

ENGLISH ORIGINS. Most of the emigrants come from southern England. They will name their new homes for towns they left behind, such as Plymouth, Boston, and Greenwich.

Areas shown are where Puritans emigrated from during the period 1620–1675.

Main areas
Secondary areas
Other

Departure from Plymouth

THE *SPEEDWELL*. The Leiden group bought this ship to sail from Holland to England and then on to America. The *Speedwell* is only a third of the size of the *Mayflower*.

Your group joins the Pilgrims from Leiden in the port of Southampton. They sailed earlier from Delfshaven in Holland aboard the *Speedwell*. With your family and fellow Pilgrims you board the *Mayflower* and, on August 15, 1620, the two ships set sail, carrying 120 passengers between them. But the *Speedwell* begins to leak and has to make for port to be repaired. At Plymouth the leaders decided to abandon the *Speedwell* and move all of the passengers onto the *Mayflower*. Upset by the bad start and crowded conditions, a number of Pilgrims give up at this point. In all, the *Mayflower* holds 102 passengers when she finally departs from Plymouth on September 16.

THE FIRST LEG. The map (right) shows the first leg of the journey, with the Leiden group sailing from Holland to Southampton. There they meet with other English Pilgrims before departing for America. But the leaking *Speedwell* forces the ships to stop for repairs at Dartmouth and Plymouth.

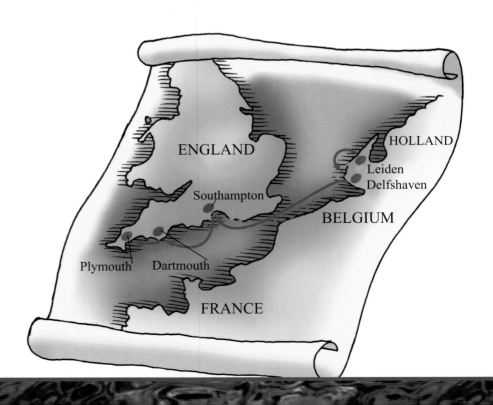

ENGLAND

HOLLAND

Leiden
Delfshaven

Southampton

BELGIUM

Plymouth   Dartmouth

FRANCE

Loading the Mayflower

THE PILGRIMS have to take with them all of the clothes, tools, and equipment they will need in the New World—there are no stores there to buy new goods from. Your father is a boot and shoe maker and dealer, and he loads 250 pairs of shoes and 13 pairs of boots onto the *Mayflower*.

The Mayflower

The 180-ton vessel is about 30 yards (27 meters) long, 9 yards (8 meters) wide, and carries sails on three masts and a bowsprit. Along with the rest of the passengers you are berthed on the gun deck, which provides protection from the weather. It is a crowded space and you and your parents use simple dividers to make a small "cabin" to give you some privacy. You spend your time preparing food and helping your mother and other mothers with young children.

CABINS
The sleeping quarters for the other crew members.

STEERAGE
Where the pilot steers the ship using a "whipstaff"—a stick that is moved back and forth to control the rudder.

POOP HOUSE
Living quarters for the captain and some of the higher-ranking crew.

MAIN DECK. In good weather the passengers can exercise on the deck. This is a welcome relief from the dark, damp, and smelly conditions of the gun deck.

GUN DECK (LIVING QUARTERS). This is where the passengers live on the *Mayflower*. It has bunks fitted to accommodate them and most family groups use blankets to make simple dividers. These provide some privacy, but it is impossible to escape from the noise and the smells of the other passengers.

HOLD
Located at the bottom of the ship, this is where the Pilgrims store food, tools, and supplies.

Handy Hint

Watch out for large waves when you use the facilities on the beakhead!

Main deck

FORECASTLE
Where the meals are prepared and the supplies stowed.

Bowsprit

BEAKHEAD
Projecting from the front of the ship, this is used for the latrines (toilets).

39

The Crew

The *Mayflower* has a crew of about 30 (only a few of whom are now known by name). The ship's master (captain) is Christopher Jones, an experienced sailor about 50 years of age. He has a stake in the voyage, as he is part-owner of the *Mayflower*. The master's mates, John Clarke and Robert Coppin, have both sailed to Virginia and New England on earlier voyages. Giles Heale is the ship's surgeon and the 21-year-old John Alden is the ship's cooper (barrel maker). Young and handsome, Alden catches your eye early on in the voyage. Later he will decide to join the Pilgrims—and eventually becomes your husband!

Important Crew Members

NAVIGATOR. He is responsible for plotting the ship's course.

HELMSMAN. He steers the *Mayflower* using the whipstaff.

SURGEON. He is responsible for the health of everyone on board.

Handy Hint

Make friends with the captain and crew—you may need their help later in the voyage!

The captain works us too hard. I might join the Pilgrims!

THE SAILMAKER maintains and repairs the ship's sails.

A GUNNER maintains and fires the ship's cannon if under attack.

COOPER. He makes and repairs barrels for storing water.

The Passengers

Who's Who

WILLIAM BREWSTER is the Pilgrims' religious leader, responsible for approval from the London Virginia Company, who agreed to resettle them in America.

William Brewster

MILES STANDISH is a professional soldier who has been hired as a military advisor to the Pilgrims.

EDWARD WINSLOW will act as a diplomat, negotiating with the Native Americans and suppliers in England.

Miles Standish

Edward Winslow

William Bradford

WILLIAM BRADFORD will eventually become the governor of the Plimoth Colony, re-elected 30 times.

The 102 passengers live in close contact with one another for 66 days. They are formed from two groups (now known as the Leiden Contingent and the London Contingent). The 41 passengers from Leiden are led by William Brewster, Edward Winslow, and William Bradford. Many of the men are adventurers, like Miles Standish, who is traveling to America to make his fortune rather than to escape religious persecution.

Wives and Children

EIGHTEEN OF THE MEN have brought their wives with them, while several have left wives behind, concerned about the dangers and hardship involved in settling in a new colony. That proves to be a wise decision, for three-quarters of the women will die by the end of the harsh first winter in the colony.

MANY FAMILIES have brought their children with them, although several decided to leave them behind with relatives, planning to send for them once the colony is set up. There are 32 children and young people on board. Aged around 17, you are the eldest of the girls. All 11 girls survive the voyage and only two will die during the first winter.

Handy Hint

Get to know the other passengers—they could help if your family become ill or die!

43

Storms and Sickness

Many of the passengers suffer from seasickness, having never been at sea before. But by October, the *Mayflower* begins to encounter storms in the mid-Atlantic and life on board ship becomes increasingly miserable. You stay belowdecks most of the time, helping your mother to prepare food and trying to keep your clothes dry. Being on deck can be risky. During one storm a Pilgrim is swept overboard, but is saved by the crew.

ROCKED BY WAVES, it is very difficult to cook and serve food. There is also the danger of fire spreading from the open ovens. In the worst weather everyone goes hungry.

SPRINGING LEAKS. The ship develops leaks, which the carpenter seals using oakum—hemp or jute fiber, treated with tar.

CRACKED BEAMS. A main beam cracks, but repairs are made using a large screw to hold the timber together.

SEASICKNESS. Most of the passengers suffer from seasickness. This weakens their resistance to other illnesses, such as pneumonia.

Life and Death on the Mayflower

You've got no stomach for the sea, that's your problem!

Three of the women on board ship were pregnant when the voyage began. Elizabeth Hopkins gives birth to a son, whom she and her husband name Oceanus. Two other women are due to give birth shortly after the *Mayflower* reaches America. You get to know these mothers and help them in caring for their new babies. But the voyage also takes its toll. One of the sailors makes fun of the Pilgrims' discomfort and seasickness. He curses them daily, saying that he hopes to throw their dead bodies overboard and take their belongings for himself. But he is then among the first to die.

FIRST PILGRIM TO DIE. William Butten, one of the passengers, becomes ill and dies three days before the *Mayflower* makes landfall.

ONE OF THE SEAMEN taunts the sick Pilgrims. William Bradford will later write "it pleased God to smite this young man with a grievous disease, of which he died in a desperate manner and so was himself the first that was thrown overboard."

Land Ahoy!

The crew spot Cape Cod as the sun begins to rise on November 9. The Atlantic storms have blown the *Mayflower* far north of her course to Virginia. At first the Pilgrim leaders decide to head south for the Hudson River (in present-day New York state). But after encountering rough seas they agree to explore the Cape Cod region instead, anchoring in what is now Provincetown Harbor. Like everyone else on the ship, you are thrilled to finally see land and glad that your family has survived the dangerous voyage. But the Pilgrim leaders have a dilemma. The land they have sighted is a long way from Virginia and they have had no rights granted to them to settle there.

LAND AT LAST. After 66 days at sea everyone is happy to see land again. But there is no one there to greet you. The land appears to be a wilderness, but Native Americans actually settled there many years earlier.

LAND AHOY! It's America!

48

Cape Cod Bay

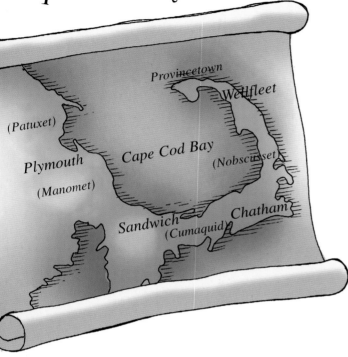

Handy Hint

Make sure your settlement is legal, otherwise it could be taken from you!

PEOPLE LIVE HERE! Although the land that the Pilgrims have sighted does not have any European settlers, there are a number of Indian tribes in the region. The map (left) shows the tribe names (in parentheses) and the names of the towns that are eventually founded around Cape Cod Bay.

The Mayflower Compact

THE PILGRIM LEADERS know that the Cape Cod region is far north of the area in which the London Virginia Company granted them a right to settle. They decide to make their colony legitimate by signing the Mayflower Compact, which sets out the laws for their colony. It is signed on November 21, 1620, by 41 of the *Mayflower*'s male passengers—including your father. Although today it is recognized as the first official document of American democracy, no women were allowed to sign it.

Exploring the Region

What Happens When You Land?

WASHING CLOTHES. You join the other women on the shore, where you wash clothes in a stream.

In the first few days after landing the men explore the immediate region on foot. The Pilgrims have brought a small boat with them to explore the coastline, but it has been damaged during the voyage. By the time it is repaired winter has set in and snow begins to fall. But on December 21 the boat enters the waters of what is to become known as Plymouth Harbor. At last a site has been found for the colony.

REPAIRING THE SHALLOP. The Pilgrims have brought a "shallop," a 30-foot single-sail boat, with them aboard the *Mayflower*. It was dismantled for the voyage, but suffered some damage. It takes several weeks to repair the boat and make her seaworthy. During this time some of the men explore on foot. The women and children remain on board the *Mayflower*— there is no shelter on the shore.

EXPLORING THE COASTLINE. Once the shallop is repaired a party of men sets out to explore the coast. Over the course of several trips they follow the coastline around Cape Cod Bay, landing at different locations in search of a site for their colony. When they enter what is now known as Plymouth Harbor they find an ideal site, with fertile soil and fresh water.

Look Out for Indians!

THE EXPLORING PARTY is led by Captain Miles Standish, a professional soldier hired by the Pilgrims as military advisor. Armed with flintlock muskets, Standish and his men are ready to protect themselves if attacked. As they explore they see Indians at a distance, but only have one dangerous encounter: one night when they are camped on the shore a band of Indians fire arrows at them. No one is injured.

Handy Hint

Explore the region carefully. You don't want to build your colony in a swamp or some other poor location!

Building Plimoth Colony

Your New Home!

YOUR FIRST SIGHT of the new colony is a shock. There is nothing there except trees and wilderness. This is the first time you understand how hard it will be to build a new life in America. At times you regret ever leaving England.

The shallop returns to the *Mayflower* with news of a good site to establish a colony—this is named Plimoth (now Plymouth) after the port that you sailed from. The *Mayflower* sails into the harbor, and in the days that follow the men begin clearing the land and marking out the sites for their houses. Like most of the other women and children you remain on the *Mayflower*, waiting for the completion of the buildings. But you are kept busy, nursing the growing number of ill people.

But it's just a wilderness!

CLEARING THE LAND. The first task is to clear the land and mark out sites for houses and other buildings. It is agreed that the men will build their own homes, but they will cooperate to build a "common house" first. This is completed by mid-January, providing somewhere warm and dry to sleep.

BUILDING HOUSES. The trees cut down to clear the land are used to build simple wood-framed houses. Dry grass and sticks are gathered to thatch the roofs. In all seven houses and four storehouses are built, along with a "gun platform," which holds the cannon the Pilgrims brought, for defense from Indians and other enemies.

Handy Hint

Build your house as quickly as you can to avoid the worst of the winter weather!

Stop shirking!

NO HOLIDAYS. The men work in all weather, even on Christmas Day. It is the end of March before everyone can move ashore. You can't wait, because by now you have been living aboard the *Mayflower* for more than six months.

A Cruel Winter, then Thanksgiving

The "Great Sickness"

FIFTY of the Pilgrims—half your number—die during the first winter. All of your family are among those who perish.

While the men work on the land, illness spreads among the women on the *Mayflower*. By the time that the houses are ready, 13 of the original 18 have died. You nurse your father, mother, and younger brother, but all of them die, leaving you an orphan. The crew sails the *Mayflower* back to England in April 1621, but the fortunes of the survivors in Plimoth begin to turn. Friendly Indians help your settlement and in the autumn the colonists and their Indian allies enjoy the first Thanksgiving meal on American soil.

Squanto

DURING MARCH the Pilgrims are visited by Squanto, a Pawtuxet Indian who speaks some English.

SQUANTO explains how he came to learn the language. He had been captured by the English in 1614.

WHEN SQUANTO REACHED ENGLAND he learned the language. He returned home in 1619. He can now help the Pilgrims to communicate with the local Indians, and also teaches them how to catch fish and grow corn.

THE INDIAN PEACE TREATY. With Squanto's help the Pilgrims negotiate a peace treaty with Massasoit, chief of the local Wampanoag Indians. They help the Pilgrims to plant and harvest crops and join them in October 1621 for their first Thanksgiving meal.

The Mayflower Legacy

In the years that follow, the colony grows and new settlements are established. You marry John Alden, the cooper from the *Mayflower*, and raise nine children. Today, your legacy and that of the other passengers aboard the *Mayflower* has spread throughout the United States. It is estimated that 35 million Americans—12 percent of the total population—are direct descendants of the *Mayflower* Pilgrims. You may have risked everything during that dangerous voyage to a new land, but your descendants now enjoy the freedom that the Pilgrims were seeking when they first set sail: beginning a voyage that, in the end, you are glad you made.

Your Descendants

YOUR FAMILY'S descendants include many famous Americans.

JOHN ADAMS (1735–1826) became the second president of the United States in 1797.

JOHN QUINCY ADAMS (1767–1848), the son of John, became the sixth president.

A THRIVING COMMUNITY. The Plimoth colony grew and prospered over the years. Today, the town of Plymouth is a popular tourist attraction. A replica of the *Mayflower* in the harbor and a reconstruction of the Plimoth Plantation attract visitors from around the world.

HENRY WADSWORTH LONGFELLOW (1807–1882), a popular and influential poet.

WILLIAM CULLEN BRYANT (1794–1878), a journalist, critic, and poet.

ORSON WELLES (1915–1985), actor/director, and MARILYN MONROE (1926–1962), actress.

57

You Wouldn't Want to Sail on a 19th-Century Whaling Ship!

Introduction

The year is 1819. You are a 14-year-old boy named Thomas Nickerson. You were born on Cape Cod, in Massachusetts, but grew up on the nearby island of Nantucket. It is one of the most important centers of the American whaling industry. In your day, whales supply two important resources: whale oil and baleen. Whale oil is used as lamp fuel and for making candles—in the early 19th century there is no electricity, gas, or kerosene for lighting. Baleen is a tough, flexible substance which comes from the mouths of some whale species. It is used to make corset stays, umbrella and parasol ribs, skirt hoops, and carriage springs. The only way to harvest whale oil and baleen is to hunt whales at sea. As you will learn, it is a bloody and dangerous business.

You want to fulfill your boyhood dream of becoming a whaler by joining your friends aboard the whaling ship *Essex*. The *Essex* is bound for the Pacific Ocean, and a place in history. But you have no idea of the horrors that lie ahead.

Nantucket: Whaling Capital of the World

Uses of Whale Oil

WHALE OIL is used to make many important items in the 19th century, such as lamp fuel, candles, margarine, shoe polish, and soap.

Nantucket is a small island located in the North Atlantic, about 25 miles (40 km) south of Cape Cod. In 1819, it is the whaling capital of the world, with a fleet of over 70 ships. You grew up playing with friends in the busy harbor as whaling ships prepared to sail. Other ships returned from long voyages with their holds filled with barrels of whale oil. You are determined to join one of these ships and earn your living as a whaler.

That's a whale of a sight!

WHALE-OIL MAN. Whale oil is delivered to your door.

WIDOW'S WALK. Some Nantucket houses have a platform on the roof where mothers and wives can watch for returning ships. Many ships do not return.

Whaling Towns

There are whaling fleets in many New England ports. The largest are at Nantucket and New Bedford.

North America

Gloucester
Marblehead
Provincetown
New London
Stonington
NEW BEDFORD
Amagansett
Edgartown
East Hampton
Southampton
NANTUCKET

Handy Hint

Get used to the smell of whale oil. You will smell plenty of this during your long voyage!

The Whaling Ship Essex

You sign up as cabin boy aboard the *Essex* for a two- to three-year voyage to the whaling grounds of the Pacific. You join three of your young friends who sign on as sailors. The 21-man crew is a mixed group of experienced whalers and "green hands," or those who have never sailed on a whaling ship before. You aren't paid wages, but have to negotiate a share, or "lay," of the future profits for the voyage. The last cabin boy's lay was about $150 for two years' work!

THE *ESSEX*. With an overall length of 87 feet (26.5 m), the *Essex* has 12 sails and carries several smaller whaleboats that are launched whenever a whale is sighted. In the center of the deck is the "try works," a brick stove that is used for "trying out," or boiling whale blubber into oil.

The Crew

IN CHARGE is Captain George Pollard. There are also two mates, three boatsteerers, a steward, 13 sailors, and a cabin boy.

The sailors include seven African Americans, one of whom deserts the ship on the outbound voyage.

Handy Hint

Take your own clothing. The captain will charge you for any clothes he supplies you with. He will charge you interest, too, and take it from your share of the profits.

A YOUNG CREW. Some of the crew on board are still boys, including you (age 14), Charles Ramsdell (age 15), Barzillai Ray (age 18), and Owen Coffin (age 17). Coffin is the captain's cousin.

THE *ESSEX* was launched in 1799. It has completed several successful whaling voyages before you sail from Nantucket harbor on August 12, 1819, with Captain Pollard's crew.

Some of the crew look scarier than the whales!

Life Aboard Ship

Your Duties

AS THE YOUNGEST crew member, you do all the odd jobs and learn what it takes to sail and maintain the *Essex*.

SWABBING DECKS. Scrub them clean. Whale's blood can be very slippery.

TIDYING ROPES. Coil them neatly—you don't want the captain to trip over one!

Right over left...

SERVING MEALS. Be quick—the captain likes his food hot.

Your ship is just 87 feet (26.5 m) long and is packed with provisions for the voyage. There are also 1,200 barrels that you hope to fill with whale oil before you return. Your duties as cabin boy include keeping the decks clean, the ropes tidy, and doing odd jobs for Captain Pollard. In your spare time, an old sailor teaches you the art of scrimshaw, which is carving intricate designs onto the teeth of sperm whales. You will soon have plenty of teeth to practice on because the *Essex*, like other Nantucket whalers, specializes in catching sperm whales.

BELOWDECKS. Living quarters are divided into three areas. The captain and the two mates have cabins at the rear. You and the white members of the crew live in the steerage section. The African American sailors occupy the forecastle at the front of the ship. The hold and the blubber room are where barrels, provisions, spare sails, and ropes are stored.

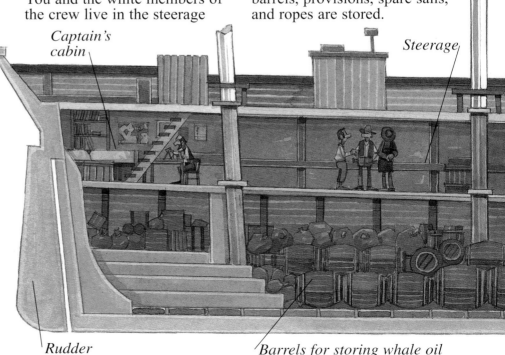

Captain's cabin

Steerage

Rudder

Barrels for storing whale oil and clean water

SCRIMSHAW. Designs are carved into the surface of a whale's tooth with a knife or a sail needle, and then filled in with lampblack (made from soot) or ink. Most of the designs are of whaling scenes, but sailors also draw their family or sweethearts.

Scrape Scrape

Handy Hint

Learn how to make scrimshaw carvings on whales' teeth. You will be able to sell your work when you return to port.

Scrimshaw designs on whale teeth

Blubber room

Try works

Forecastle

Hold

FOLK CRAFT ANTIQUES. Today good scrimshaws are very collectable, and many are housed in museum collections.

65

The Whaling Grounds: Pacific vs. Arctic

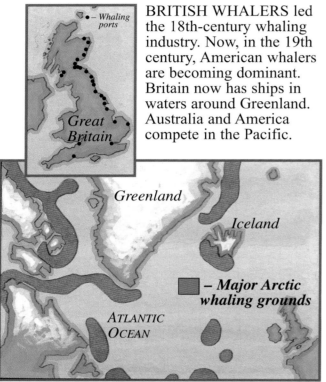

Whaling ports

Great Britain

Greenland

Iceland

ATLANTIC OCEAN

— Major Arctic whaling grounds

BRITISH WHALERS led the 18th-century whaling industry. Now, in the 19th century, American whalers are becoming dominant. Britain now has ships in waters around Greenland. Australia and America compete in the Pacific.

he *Essex* competes with many whaling ships from America and Australia. British fleets mainly hunt baleen whales in the Arctic, where the ships risk being trapped in the pack ice. In 1819, the year the *Essex* sets sail, ten British ships are lost in the ice. You are fortunate that the *Essex* is heading for the warm Pacific seas. Your captain steers a southerly course down the South American coast, around Cape Horn, and into the Pacific Ocean.

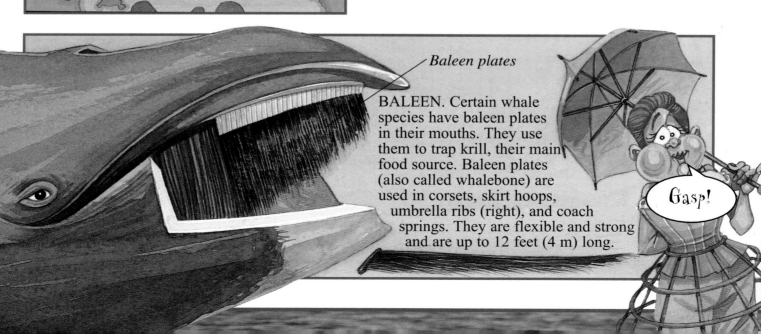

Baleen plates

BALEEN. Certain whale species have baleen plates in their mouths. They use them to trap krill, their main food source. Baleen plates (also called whalebone) are used in corsets, skirt hoops, umbrella ribs (right), and coach springs. They are flexible and strong and are up to 12 feet (4 m) long.

Gasp!

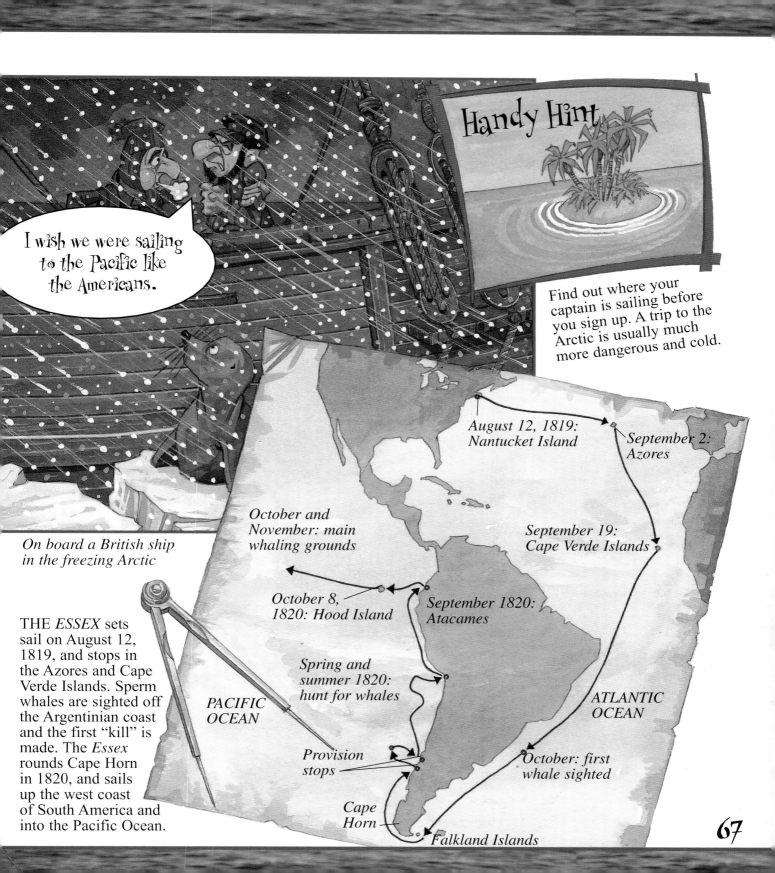

I wish we were sailing to the Pacific like the Americans.

On board a British ship in the freezing Arctic

Handy Hint

Find out where your captain is sailing before you sign up. A trip to the Arctic is usually much more dangerous and cold.

THE *ESSEX* sets sail on August 12, 1819, and stops in the Azores and Cape Verde Islands. Sperm whales are sighted off the Argentinian coast and the first "kill" is made. The *Essex* rounds Cape Horn in 1820, and sails up the west coast of South America and into the Pacific Ocean.

August 12, 1819: Nantucket Island

September 2: Azores

September 19: Cape Verde Islands

October and November: main whaling grounds

October 8, 1820: Hood Island

September 1820: Atacames

Spring and summer 1820: hunt for whales

PACIFIC OCEAN

ATLANTIC OCEAN

October: first whale sighted

Provision stops

Cape Horn

Falkland Islands

There She Blows!

The *Essex* has been at sea for over three months when the lookout cries, "There she blows!" He means that he has spotted a whale's spout, which is the spray of moist, warm air released from a whale's blowhole when it surfaces to breathe. You hope it's a sperm whale. Most experienced whalers can tell different whale species by the size and shape of the whale's spout. The crew lowers the three whaleboats over the side, leaving just three "shipkeepers" aboard the *Essex*. You take an oar in a whaleboat and begin to row with the rest of the crew toward the pod of whales, now about a mile away.

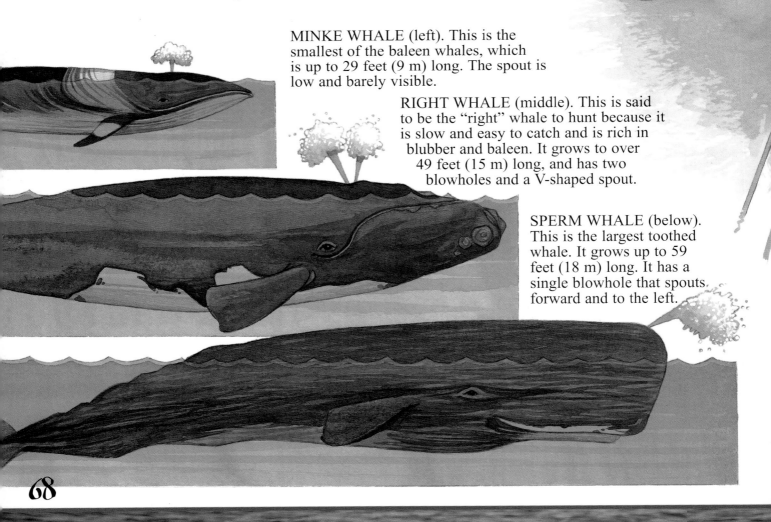

MINKE WHALE (left). This is the smallest of the baleen whales, which is up to 29 feet (9 m) long. The spout is low and barely visible.

RIGHT WHALE (middle). This is said to be the "right" whale to hunt because it is slow and easy to catch and is rich in blubber and baleen. It grows to over 49 feet (15 m) long, and has two blowholes and a V-shaped spout.

SPERM WHALE (below). This is the largest toothed whale. It grows up to 59 feet (18 m) long. It has a single blowhole that spouts forward and to the left.

There she blows!

Handy Hint

Learn to distinguish between the spouts of different whale species. Some are much more valuable than others.

SEI WHALE. This streamlined whale grows to 49 feet (15 m) long. Its spout looks like a cone.

SOUTHERN BOTTLE-NOSED WHALE (below). This 23-foot (7-m)-long toothed whale has a bushy spout.

HUMPBACK WHALE (right). This whale reaches a length of over 49 feet (15 m). Its spout makes a wide arc that rises about 13 feet (4 m) in the air.

THE CAPTAIN'S log book records different whale species and how many barrels of oil they produce. Vertical sketches show escaped whales and horizontal ones show those that are killed.

DIVING PATTERNS. Whalers predict where a sperm whale will surface based on the number of times it "blows" before diving. The whale usually blows once for each minute it will spend underwater.

DIVE BEGINS. The whale takes a final breath before diving.

INTO THE DEPTHS. Sperm whales can dive as deep as 6,562 feet (2,000 m).

UP FOR AIR. Most whales dive for 10–20 minutes, but sperm whales can stay submerged for up to 2 hours!

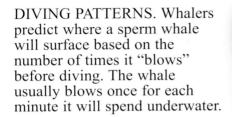

A Nantucket Sleigh Ride

The crew fails to catch a whale at the first sighting. A few days later, a sperm whale is harpooned and you take your first "Nantucket sleigh ride." Your whaleboat is dragged behind the whale at speeds of up to 23 mph (37 kmh). This weakens the whale until it lies exhausted on the surface. The boatsteerer then spears it with his "killing lance." The dying whale's spout turns red with blood and the crew cries out "Chimney's afire!"

On Board the Whaleboat

ROW STEADY. With the boatsteerer at the bow of the boat, you approach the floating whale.

GIVE IT TO HIM! He throws the harpoon into the side of the whale.

Whoosh

Hold on to your hats!

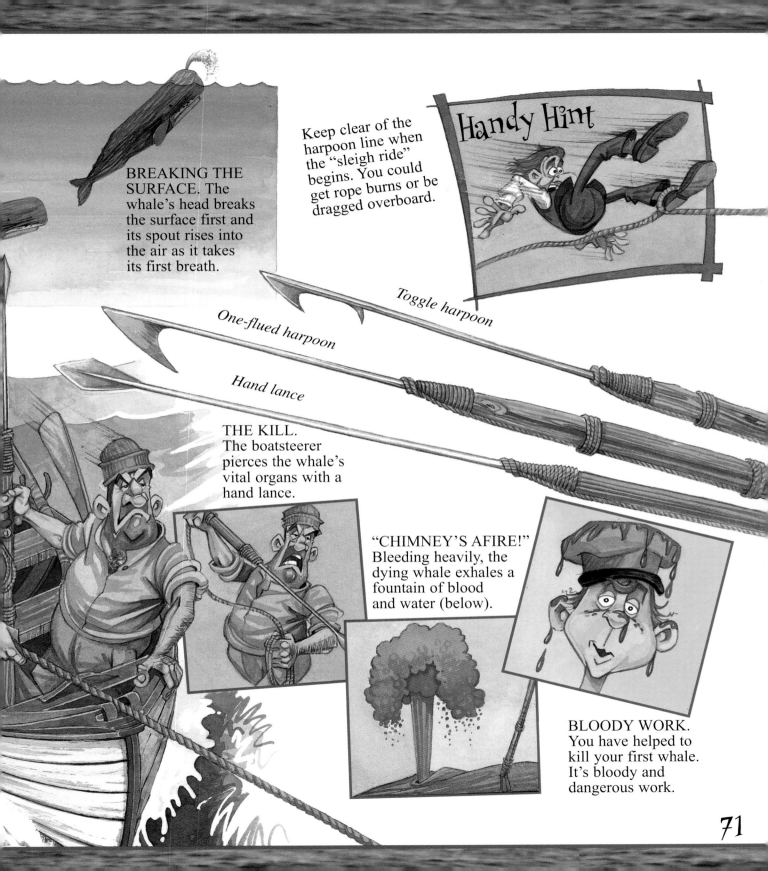

BREAKING THE SURFACE. The whale's head breaks the surface first and its spout rises into the air as it takes its first breath.

Keep clear of the harpoon line when the "sleigh ride" begins. You could get rope burns or be dragged overboard.

Handy Hint

Toggle harpoon

One-flued harpoon

Hand lance

THE KILL. The boatsteerer pierces the whale's vital organs with a hand lance.

"CHIMNEY'S AFIRE!" Bleeding heavily, the dying whale exhales a fountain of blood and water (below).

BLOODY WORK. You have helped to kill your first whale. It's bloody and dangerous work.

"Flensing" the Whale

The whale is towed back to the *Essex* where the crew tie it to the ship. A platform called the "cutting stage" is hung over its body. The captain and mate strip the blubber (the fatty layer below the skin) from the whale's body. This is called "flensing." A large hook is inserted behind the whale's front fin. This is attached with ropes and chains to a system of pulleys. A strip of blubber about 5 feet (1.5 m) wide is cut around the whale's body. The crew pull at the ropes until the hook pulls away a long strip of blubber. This "blanket piece" weighs about a ton and will be cut into sections.

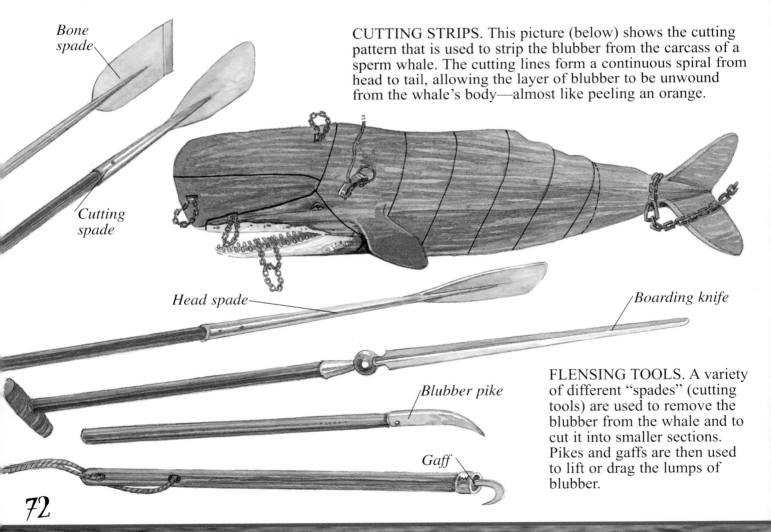

Bone spade

Cutting spade

Head spade

Blubber pike

Gaff

Boarding knife

CUTTING STRIPS. This picture (below) shows the cutting pattern that is used to strip the blubber from the carcass of a sperm whale. The cutting lines form a continuous spiral from head to tail, allowing the layer of blubber to be unwound from the whale's body—almost like peeling an orange.

FLENSING TOOLS. A variety of different "spades" (cutting tools) are used to remove the blubber from the whale and to cut it into smaller sections. Pikes and gaffs are then used to lift or drag the lumps of blubber.

72

"Trying Out" the Oil

The Process

DRAINING.
A hole is cut in the whale's skull to drain the spermaceti. As much as 528 gallons (2,000 l) can be harvested from a large whale.

PULLING TEETH. Ropes and pulleys are used to pull the whale's teeth from its jawbone.

HORSE PIECES.
The long strips of whale blubber are carved into smaller blocks known as the "horse pieces."

With the blubber removed, the sperm whale's head is cut from its body and raised onto the deck. The spermaceti (liquid wax) and teeth are removed from the head.
Now it's time to "try out" the oil from the whale's blubber. Fires are lit in the try pots, and sections of blubber are lowered inside. The fatty blubber boils and is turned into oil, which is poured into barrels. The bloody carcass of the whale drifts away from the boat, where sharks and seabirds will eat what is left.

SPERMACETI.
Located in the skull, the spermaceti organ is unique to the sperm whale. Its liquid wax is valuable to whalers, who use it to make high-quality candles.

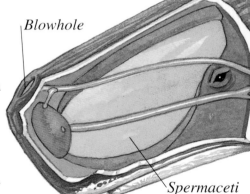

Blowhole

Spermaceti

Tool for cutting bible leaves

THIN SLICES are cut from the horse pieces (left). These are called "bible leaves" because they flop open like the pages of a book. They are put into the "try pots" (right). The blubber melts into oil, which is skimmed off the surface, cooled, and drained into barrels.

Rammed by a Whale!

The months go by as you search for whales in the middle of the Pacific Ocean. It is November 20, 1820, a day you will remember for the rest of your life. While most of the crew are on a whale hunt, you spot a huge sperm whale heading straight for the *Essex*. First it rams the ship's side. Then it rams the bow, pushing the ship backward and causing seawater to pour into the hold. The *Essex* begins to sink. The whale swims away, leaving the wreckage of the ship and its crew to the mercy of the Pacific Ocean.

SHIPKEEPER It's your turn to stay on the *Essex* as a shipkeeper. Most of the crew take the three whaleboats.

DAMAGED. The first mate's whaleboat is damaged by a whale during the chase and returns to the *Essex* for repairs.

YOUR JOURNAL. Many years later you write a journal with drawings of the whale attack and the sinking of the *Essex*. You write, "Here lay our beautiful ship, a floating and dismal wreck..."

LOOK OUT! A huge whale, about 85 feet (26 m) long and weighing 80 tons, is heading for the *Essex*. Does it see the ship as a rival male?

HAMMERING. Maybe the bull (male) sperm whale was attracted by the sound of the crew repairing the ship.

Alone in the Pacific

The other two whaleboats return to the sinking ship. The first mate tells the captain how the *Essex* has been rammed by a whale. You help the crew save some of the supplies aboard the ship before it sinks beneath the waves. With no hope of rescue, Captain Pollard decides to sail the three whaleboats to the coast of South America, which is 2,983 miles (4,800 km) away. Your daily rations are limited to 6 ounces (170 g) of hardtack biscuit and a quart (1 liter) of water per man, plus whatever fish you can catch. You may have enough supplies for a two-month voyage. Will the food and water last?

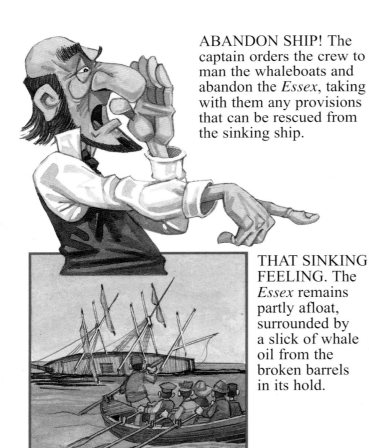

ABANDON SHIP! The captain orders the crew to man the whaleboats and abandon the *Essex*, taking with them any provisions that can be rescued from the sinking ship.

THAT SINKING FEELING. The *Essex* remains partly afloat, surrounded by a slick of whale oil from the broken barrels in its hold.

SHORT RATIONS. Two casks of bread, 595 pounds (270 kg) of hardtack biscuits, and several casks of fresh water are rescued from the ship. There are barely enough rations for 20 men to share.

TORTOISE STEAKS. The giant tortoises that were caught earlier in the voyage swim to the whaleboats from the wreck. All are cooked in their shells and eaten.

CANNIBALS? The nearest land is the Marquesa Islands, but the captain heads for South America. The crew think that cannibals live on the islands and that they would be eaten if they landed there. They are wrong, however, and this decision will have grim results.

Handy Hint

Remember to rescue the ship's quadrant so you can find your position. Without it, you cannot sail a correct course to land.

KILLER WHALE ATTACK. About a week after the crew abandon the *Essex*, a killer whale attacks the whaleboat under Captain Pollard's command. It bites a chunk out of the side of the boat and beats the vessel with its tail before the crew drive the whale off.

Pick on someone your own size!

Starvation, Madness, and Cannibalism

After surviving for a month on little food and water, you finally sight land. It is a small deserted island that cannot support 20 men. Three stay on the island and the rest of the crew set sail again. Within days, the three boats are separated in a storm. One is never seen again. As weaker crew members die from thirst and hunger, the survivors turn to cannibalism to survive. Finally, after 90 days, your boat is sighted. You are saved, but 12 of the crew have died, including two of your friends.

Essex rammed by whale, November 20, 1820

Attack by killer whale

PACIFIC OCEAN

South American coast

Land on Henderson Island, December 20

Second mate dies

Four men die

Pollard's route

Chase rescued

Chase's route

Coffin killed

Pollard rescued

Life Adrift

LAND HO! On December 20, you sight Henderson Island. It has no inhabitants and little food for the hungry crew.

HE'S MINE! The men search for fresh water and food. They find water and catch crabs, fish, and birds.

I want the claws!

Don't forget us!

STAYING BEHIND. The captain knows that the island can't support 20 men, so three stay behind.

The Fate of Owen Coffin

On Captain Pollard's boat, only he and your three friends are left alive. They agree to draw straws over who should die to feed the others. Owen Coffin, the Captain's cousin, draws the "short straw" and is killed by his best friend, Charles Ramsdell. Pollard later recalls, "He was soon dispatched, and nothing of him left."

Handy Hint

Don't throw your dead shipmates overboard. If you have no other choice, you may be forced to eat one of them just to survive.

BONES. The captain and Ramsdell survive by sucking bone marrow from the dead.

SEPARATED IN A STORM. After leaving the island, a storm separates the three whaleboats. You are in the boat of First Mate Owen Chase.

FIRST DEATH. On January 10 the second mate, Matthew Joy, dies. His body is lowered into the ocean.

GOING MAD. Driven almost mad by thirst and hunger, the survivors decide to eat their dead friends to stay alive.

RESCUED. On February 18, 1821, you are rescued by the ship *Indian*. Pollard and Ramsdell are found five days later.

81

The Homecoming

Eight out of the twenty crew members survive the voyage of the *Essex*: three on board your boat, two on Captain Pollard's boat, and the three men left on Henderson Island. You and the others in the boats turned to cannibalism to survive. News of this spreads through the ports of North America. Several months pass before you return to Nantucket, but not to a hero's welcome. More than 1,500 people gather for the arrival of Captain Pollard. As he makes his way home, the silent crowd parts to let him pass. After all, he has eaten his cousin!

MOBY-DICK (below). The story of the *Essex* inspired Herman Melville's famous novel *Moby-Dick*. Published in 1851, it is the story of Captain Ahab's search for a giant white sperm whale, which eventually kills him and his crew.

YOU become a merchant captain and write a story about your adventure. It lies undiscovered for almost 100 years, but is published in 1984.

Why are they looking at us like that?

Whaling Now

TODAY, some countries have signed agreements not to hunt whales. There are alternatives to the oil and the baleen that the large whale species once provided.

Whales are now endangered species. However, some countries continue to hunt them. In 1910, about 12,300 whales were killed, and in 2001, 1,500 were killed.

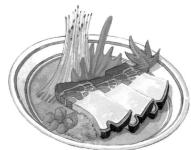

Whale meat is a great delicacy in some countries

WHALE WATCHING.
In Nantucket, whales are viewed on trips from the harbor (right). There is also a museum where visitors can explore the gruesome past of whaling and the story of the *Essex*.

Whale watching in Nantucket

You Wouldn't Want to Sail on an Irish Famine Ship!

Introduction

ou are Brian Walsh, a farmer living in the west of Ireland in the 1840s. It's hard work feeding your family and paying rent to your landlord, but Ireland is a peaceful and beautiful place. Then in 1845 everything changes. There have been famines before, but nothing like this. Year after year, a mystery disease wipes out your potato crop—your main source of food.

Your landlord lives in England. He's more worried about the rent than about his starving tenants. To escape the horrors of the famine, you make up your mind to travel 3,100 miles (5,000 km) across the Atlantic in the hope of starting a new life with your family. You'll be packed like sardines into a leaky, stinking ship. You must endure seasickness, storms, a vicious crew, rotten food, unsafe water, and worst of all, the deadly "black fever."

During the famine—also known as the "Great Hunger"—one million Irish emigrants sailed across the Atlantic, while another million died at home from starvation and fever.

CANADA

Grosse Isle

Quebec

New York

USA

County Mayo (You live here)

GREAT BRITAIN

Dublin

IRELAND

Liverpool

Your whole family lives on a small patch of land, growing row after row of potatoes.

Scratching Out a Living

THE WEST COAST. Like most people here, you live off the land. It's hard to grow anything in the rocky, boggy ground. Seaweed improves the soil, but it weighs a ton!

POTATOES. Potatoes are the only crop that's easy to grow in the poor soil where you live. Luckily, they are very nutritious. One in three people in Ireland eat almost nothing but potatoes.

OUT IN THE STICKS. Like most country folk, you've never been more than a few miles from home. Yet many visitors to Ireland notice how kind local people are to passing strangers.

Before the Famine

You spend much of your time working for your landlord. Rents are high—but make sure you pay on time! Your landlord wants an excuse to get rid of you so he can use the land for sheep. Not that you ever see him—he spends most of his time in London, where he is an MP (Member of Parliament).

By the 1840s, Britain, a largely Protestant country, has ruled Ireland, a mainly Catholic country, for 600 years.* The Irish have rebelled many times, but they stand little chance against the British army. After each rebellion, the British grab more land from the Catholic Irish and give it to their Protestant supporters. In the 17th century, the British kicked Catholics off their land in the northern part of Ireland and replaced them with Protestant settlers from Scotland.

See note on page 141.

Help yourself to potatoes.

Under British law, life is hard for Catholics. Until 1829, most Irish people couldn't buy land, vote, go to church, carry a sword, or own a horse worth over five pounds.

Out of my way, slowpoke!

Handy Hint

That pig you're raising may look delicious, but it's not for eating— selling it will pay a big part of the rent.

That rat is after our food.

HOME, SWEET HOME? Your cottage is an old cowshed. It has no windows, just a hole in the roof to let the smoke out. A fire in the middle of the room keeps you warm. You share your home with chickens, ducks, and a pig.

Just like our landlord!

The Workhouse

ne rainy day in August 1845, you notice an awful stench in the air. When you dig up your potatoes, some are healthy, but many are black and slimy. All across Ireland, fields of potatoes are turning into a stinking, rotting mess. A third of the crop is lost. Luckily you have enough potatoes to get through the winter. By the following spring, however, some of your neighbors have already run out of food. They head reluctantly for the dreaded workhouses. Built to house the poor and homeless, workhouses are damp, filthy, and crowded. The food they serve is often rotten, but at least you're not starving.

WHAT'S HAPPENED?
Experts have no idea why the potatoes are rotting. They blame the cold weather, heavy summer rains, insects, and poison in the air. When they finally figure out that a fungus is making the potatoes rot, they're 30 years too late.

What Else Is There to Eat?

Ouch!

He can't be serious?

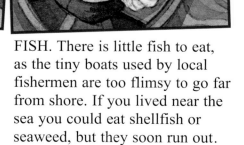

NETTLES. Nuts, dandelions, roots, mushrooms, berries, and stinging nettles are all edible, but many can be picked only at certain times of year.

MEAT. Dogs, donkeys, horses, and any wild birds you can catch would make a good meal. If you had a cow you could drain two quarts of blood from it without weakening it much; mix this with vegetables.

FISH. There is little fish to eat, as the tiny boats used by local fishermen are too flimsy to go far from shore. If you lived near the sea you could eat shellfish or seaweed, but they soon run out.

Handy Hint
Some parents sneak out of the workhouse to look for paid work. They know that the children they are leaving behind will be fed while they are away.

Do you mind if I shut the window?

With what?

TRAPPED! Workhouses are places where the poor are offered food and shelter when they have nowhere else to go. But they are like prisons. Once you enter, you cannot leave. You work all day at boring jobs such as knitting or breaking rocks into stones.

Families are torn apart, as men are forced to live in different buildings from their wives and children. The rules are very strict: there is no answering back. All meals must be eaten in silence.

The Great Hunger

What Can You Do?

 y the summer of 1846, thousands of people in your area are starving. Some villages are already deserted. The British government sets up stores all over Ireland to sell corn, but it's too expensive for poor farmers like you. Crowds gather outside the workhouses, begging for food.

The government starts lending money to landlords, so they can pay poor people to do useful jobs like mending roads. But you wait months while the paperwork is sorted out. Things go from bad to worse. The winter of 1846–47 is bitterly cold. Whole families are found dead in their cottages. In the spring, free soup kitchens are set up outside workhouses. They hand out bowls of "stirabout," a watery soup made from meal, water, and rice.

Soup kitchens will feed your family, but you feel ashamed to be standing in line with a bowl in your hand. Some soup kitchens feed you only if you promise to become a Protestant!

Eat it up, man. It'll do you good.

Will it?

FULL UP! In one workhouse, 150 boys have to share 24 beds. By 1847, people are dying inside the workhouses as they run out of food.

GUILTY! Anyone caught stealing is shipped to Australia. Some are so desperate for food that they commit petty crimes; at least in prison they will be fed.

RIOT. Watching friends and relatives wither away is enough to make you riot, but there are too many British soldiers around.

KEEP TRYING. In 1846 the potato crop is healthy, but you've already had to eat the seed potatoes needed to plant next year's crop.

Handy Hint

If you're lucky enough to get work, beware of "gombeen men" who offer to lend you money while you are waiting to be paid. They'll rip you off!

PRIME MINISTER Robert Peel buys $500,000 worth of maize to send to Ireland. But many British MPs do not want to help—they believe the landlords in Ireland should pay for the emergency food. When help does come, it's too little, too late. By 1847 three million Irish people are starving. Some drop dead as they stand in line at the soup kitchens.

Get Out!

That was our home!

In early 1847, disease breaks out all over Ireland. The hospitals cannot cope, but the British parliament leaves it to the landlords to deal with the problem. Some try to help, but many others kick starving tenants off their land for not paying the rent. Teams of "wreckers" smash down doors with axes, then take cottages apart stone by stone.

Families are forced to live by the roadside. Many die of cold. Some huddle together in shallow holes covered with sticks or turf. That spring, the fungus destroys the potato crop again. When you visit your landlord's agent he offers you tickets to America if you leave your land. You accept: it's your only hope.

Why Go to America?

Next!

DEATH. During the famine, 1.5 million Irish people die. To cope with the numbers, bodies are buried using "sliding coffins." The bottom of the coffin opens, dropping the body into a large pit. Then the coffin can be used again.

EVICTION. Between 1849 and 1854, some 49,000 families are thrown out of their homes. In Mayo, your county on the west coast, thousands of homeless families die by the side of the road.

If we weren't doing this job, we'd be evicted too.

Handy Hint

It's dangerous to fight back. Rebels in Tipperary trap the police in a cottage in the middle of widow McCormack's cabbage patch. Fighting goes on for several hours. But when more police arrive, the rebels are forced to flee.

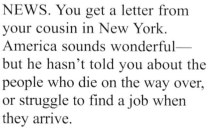

NEWS. You get a letter from your cousin in New York. America sounds wonderful—but he hasn't told you about the people who die on the way over, or struggle to find a job when they arrive.

JAIL. After 1848, anyone who protests can be thrown in jail. Troops are everywhere. The British are afraid of an uprising, but ordinary Irish people are too spread out and weak to rebel.

The Famine Ship

Most ships going to America leave from Dublin, on the east coast of Ireland. Your family must walk hundreds of miles to get there. It could be worse; many people are dying on the road. Others cannot afford to pay for the journey to England, let alone America. Most of your village is emigrating, so at least you'll be with friends.

You arrive in Dublin exhausted but alive. The quays are busy with the sound of horses' hooves and the shouts of dockers unloading cargo. Ticket in hand, you join a line of famine victims that stretches 2 miles (3 km) from the docks. There is little time for tears or farewells; you are herded like cattle onto the ships. You carry a few bags and pots and pans for cooking, but very little else.

SHIPSHAPE? Over five years, 5,000 ships sail across the Atlantic with Irish emigrants. Many are leaky old hulks that have been patched up in a hurry by owners hoping to make a quick buck. The *Elizabeth and Sarah* has been afloat for 83 years!

All Aboard!

HEALTHY? Your whole family must pass a medical examination and get their tickets stamped.

LATE! If you're late, run to the dock gate, fling your luggage onboard, and jump—hopefully you'll land on deck. A man in a rowboat waits below for anyone who misses!

BAG CHECK. Once the trip is underway, your bags are inspected. Any stowaways are returned to shore.

> Say "Ah!"

Handy Hint
If you can't afford a ticket, try to charm your way on board. In Cork, a sea captain took pity on Patrick Crotty and hired him for the voyage.

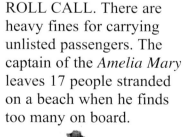

BRACE YOURSELF. People are pulled on board in a heap. Even if you fall flat on your face, the next person is pulled on top of you!

ROLL CALL. There are heavy fines for carrying unlisted passengers. The captain of the *Amelia Mary* leaves 17 people stranded on a beach when he finds too many on board.

Bon Voyage

n board, you learn that the ship is going to Canada, not New York as you were promised—because it's cheaper to sail to Canada! And the ship is stopping in Liverpool, England. Some passengers are too poor to travel any farther and end up staying there.

After a couple of days, you board the ship again. Several passengers have had their bags stolen. You're given a tiny space to live in. Luckily, you have only three children; there are nine in the family next to you. Not everyone is poor. Some can afford a cabin. The crossing usually takes 40–45 days, but due to storms, one ship, the *Industry,* takes 106 days to reach America, and 17 people starve to death on the way.

RULES. If you break the ship's rules, you risk being beaten by the crew or lashed with rope.

One rule is that you can't wash clothes on a Sunday.

You with the clean shirt—that's 20 lashes!

Life Onboard

THE CAPTAIN'S WORD is law. If passengers complain, they can be charged with mutiny—punishable by hanging!

STOWAWAYS. If stowaways appear once the ship is out to sea, some captains refuse to give them rations. To stay alive, they'll have to beg food from the other passengers.

Handy Hint

It's easy to get bored on board. Dancing and singing help to keep spirits up, but as the voyage goes on, you may not have the strength for this.

What have we here, then?

HOLD YOUR NOSE! Most of the time passengers are kept belowdecks. The only place to pour your waste is into the hold below. The smell makes it hard to breathe. The sailors are supposed to do the cleaning, but often leave it to passengers.

SLEEP TIGHT! On the *Elizabeth and Sarah*, most of the wooden bunks collapse soon after the ship sets off. Passengers have to sleep on the floor.

Staying Alive

You're allowed on deck to cook your meals using fire boxes—wooden boxes lined with bricks. Often there isn't enough fuel to cook your food properly, but any food is welcome after the horrors of the famine. Each week you are supposed to get 7 pounds (3 kg) of bread, crackers, flour, rice, oatmeal, and potatoes, but on your ship people get only half this amount. You can earn more food by working as a crew member, but you'll get beaten if you make a mistake. Each day you also get a gallon (5 liters) of water. You must line up behind a white line, and if you cross it by mistake, you lose your ration.

FIRE! Cooking on deck is risky: 9,000 emigrants die from onboard fires. If you are forced to abandon ship, there are few if any lifeboats. When the *Ocean Monarch* catches fire just 25 miles (40 km) from Liverpool, 170 passengers die.

HARD CHEESE. On some ships the only rations are moldy crackers. Cross your fingers and hope that some of the passengers know how to catch fish when you get near the Canadian coast.

STEALING. Forget it! Thieves are flayed with a whip known as the cat-o'-nine-tails. On one ship, when passengers try to break into the food storeroom, the captain threatens them with a musket.

ORDER. Fights can break out between violent passengers. On most ships the passengers elect a committee to make up rules and settle arguments.

Some rules do make sense. Don't smoke belowdecks—some ships are carrying gunpowder for the British government!

FIRE SAFETY.
At the end of the set meal times, a cabin boy nicknamed "Jack in the Shrouds" puts out fires by pouring water on the fire boxes below.

Couldn't you wait till it's cooked?

Stormy Weather

The wind is one of your only friends, speeding you to Canada, but it can also be your greatest enemy. During a storm, the hatches are shut and passengers are trapped down below, sometimes in complete darkness. You cling tightly to your children to keep them from being flung about. It's terrifying. Storm winds can blow a ship off course or force it to turn back. They also force the crew to lower the sails, slowing down the ship. In 1848 the *Creole* limps back into Cork after spending three weeks at sea. It has lost most of its sails and two masts after being struck by lightning.

Keeping Your Head in a Storm

TOSSED ABOUT. During a storm, anything not tied down gets thrown from one side to the other: people, boxes, barrels, and even dead bodies, all in one big heap.

GET ON TOP. Make sure you're in the top bunk. It's not much fun if the people above you are seasick.

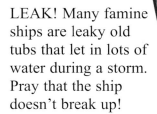

LEAK! Many famine ships are leaky old tubs that let in lots of water during a storm. Pray that the ship doesn't break up!

Should we have stayed at home?

Handy Hint

Avoid a winter crossing if you can —that's the time of the worst storms. The short days and long nights make the voyage even more depressing.

SQUASHED.
In a bad storm, the captain of the *Londonderry* forces all 174 passengers into a small cabin; 72 people are crushed or suffocated.

I can't stay like this till we get to Canada...

IN A FIX. As the ship rolls about, gaps open and close between the planks. These can trap passengers' clothing, especially women's skirts. You could be pinned down for hours.

SWEPT AWAY. If you do make it up onto the deck, there's a good chance you'll be swept away by the waves.

101

Iceberg!

After several days of stormy weather, the hatches are opened and passengers can go on deck in small groups. It's good to get away from the terrible stench below. Some of the children play catch on deck. But the danger isn't over yet—you could still be shipwrecked!

On a clear day, icebergs can be spotted through a telescope—but not in thick fog. During the five famine years (1845–49), 50 ships sink after hitting icebergs or rocks. Icebergs can be more than two-thirds of a mile (1 km) long and 200 feet (60 m) high. It's one more hazard for poor emigrants on their way to a new life.

On the Lookout!

WHALES are seen as a sign of bad luck by the crew. Dolphins and flying fish are also common sights on Atlantic crossings. Sharks often follow ships in the hope of finding a tasty morsel…

LIQUID FIRE. At night, tiny luminous creatures in the water make the ship look as if it is gliding on liquid fire—though only passengers who can afford cabins can see this.

GOING AGROUND. In 1850 the *Constitution* sailing from Belfast runs aground just after sighting land. Luckily, passengers escape to shore using a web of ropes.

SLOBS are slimy objects that float in the water. Some look like a lemon cut in half. You may also see jellyfish or Portuguese man-of-wars.

When you're up on deck it's worth scanning the horizon. A flock of birds is a good sign that land is near. Hooray!

You don't usually see them this far north.

When the Hannah strikes an iceberg the sailors jump into a lifeboat, leaving the passengers to die. But the ship takes 40 minutes to sink, giving the passengers time to climb onto the iceberg. They huddle together for 15 hours, some wearing only their nightshirts, until another ship comes to the rescue. Though 129 people are saved, many freeze to death and others are crushed by the shifting ice.

The "Coffin Ships"

You're just beginning to enjoy a spell of good weather when there's trouble on board. One of the passengers has died of fever, and in the cramped spaces belowdecks it spreads like wildfire.

Being shut up in the dark with fever victims makes some passengers panic. The terrible moans of sick people keep you awake all night.

Many emigrants are still weak from the lack of food and cannot fight the fever. Children and the elderly are most at risk. It is heartbreaking to see people dying so close to the shores of Canada.

OVERBOARD. The fever can affect people's minds. Some victims jump off the ship in a frenzy.

No Escape!

Are we there yet?

Yecch!!

SKELETON CREW!
The crew of the *Looshtauk* goes down with fever. Only the captain and first mate are healthy enough to sail the ship, with help from passengers.

WIPED OUT. When the *Virginius* arrives in America, 158 people have died since leaving Ireland and another 106 are ill with fever. Only eight people on board are still healthy at the end of the voyage.

DIRTY WATER. The fever isn't helped by the fact that after several weeks at sea, the drinking water turns bad and isn't safe to drink.

There are several deaths every day. Bodies are wrapped in sailcloth and thrown overboard. Out of 4,500 passengers who were headed to Montreal, Canada, in July 1847, more than 800 have died on the way and another 800 are sick with fever. No wonder people call these boats "coffin ships."

The Island of Death

The sight of other ships means the coast is near. Your ship must now safely navigate upriver to reach port. The next day the fog clears. Everyone who can rushes on deck. There's land on both sides! But your hopes are soon dashed. Because of the fever, all passengers must now pass a medical inspection before being ferried to Quebec. Another 20 vessels are lined up along the river, all waiting their turn. The inspection takes place on Grosse Isle, a rocky island just 3 miles (5 km) long and a mile (1.5 km) wide. Its hospital is unable to cope. After a few weeks, hordes of emigrants are sent inland, taking the fever with them. By a miracle, everyone in your family is still alive.

The Horrors of Grosse Isle

FLOATING CORPSES. Most ships are full of the ill and the dying. Many ships dump bodies overboard.

NO AMBULANCE. There is a stream of small boats carrying emigrants to shore. The sick are flung onto the beach. Many crawl up to the hospital—if they can.

FULL UP. Within two weeks of your arrival, there are 850 patients in the tiny hospital, 500 more ill with fever, and 13,000 waiting on ships to be examined. Tents are hastily put up, but proper quarantine is impossible. The sick and the healthy are put together and the fever spreads again. If you survive, you'll never forget the moans of the dying.

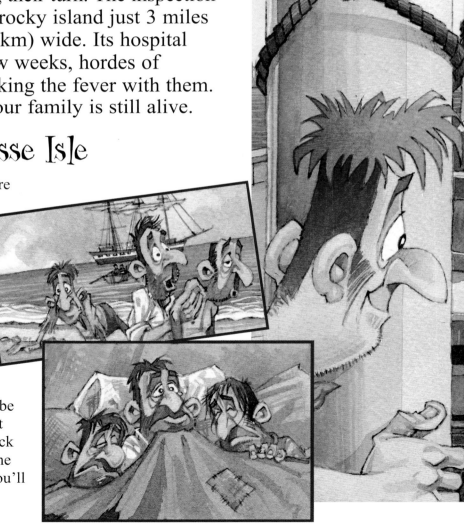

Emigrants cheer at the sight of land—but for many the first two weeks in Canada turn into a nightmare. Around 7,000 are buried at Grosse Isle.

Handy Hint

Don't be fooled if people suffering from fever suddenly seem to cheer up and start chatting. Sadly, that is usually a sign that they are about to die.

We've made it!

New York

YOU'VE LANDED in Canada, but almost half of all Irish emigrants sail to New York—during the famine years more than 650,000 arrive on 2,743 voyages. These people usually fare better than those sailing to Canada. There are stricter rules for U.S. ships, and passengers are fed better.

Journey's End

Quebec was originally a French colony, so there are few jobs for people who don't speak French. So, like most Irish emigrants, you head south for the United States. It's a long journey on foot. By the time you arrive in New York, you're exhausted. But America is a good place to be if you can work with your hands. Your wife gets a job as a servant in a rich home, and you become one of many Irishmen working on the railroads. You will never forget the famine or the coffin ships, but you and your family have survived the hunger and fever to build a new life America.

COLD. At least your family traveled in summer—15,000 emigrants will freeze to death while journeying through the harsh North American winter.

Keep Your Wits About You!

EASY PICKINGS. The docks are swarming with "runners." Some wear bright green waistcoats to attract Irish emigrants. They will either steal your luggage or carry it to a boarding house and demand an outrageous fee.

TRULY AWFUL. Some runners sell fake railroad tickets across the United States. When one man refuses to buy a ticket from "Awful" Gardner, Gardner breaks his jaw!

N.I.N.A. Irish emigrants are not always welcome: they are often poor, and many carry the fever with them. Many job advertisements say, "No Irish Need Apply."

TOUGH WORK. Many emigrants fall ill because they start work while they are still weak from the crossing. Others are forced to accept dangerous jobs, such as laying explosives to blast a path for railroads.

The Irish in America

By 1850 there were more Irish in New York than in Dublin, the capital of Ireland. Today, some 44 million Americans are of Irish heritage.

Carmaker Henry Ford was a direct descendant of a Great Famine emigrant. Presidents John F. Kennedy, Richard Nixon, Ronald Reagan, and George W. Bush all had Irish ancestors, as did pioneer Daniel Boone, playwright Eugene O'Neill, and film star John Wayne.

John F. Kennedy

Ronald Reagan

George W. Bush

You Wouldn't Want to Sail on the Titanic!

Introduction

The year is 1907. Your name is J. Bruce Ismay, and you are the managing director of the White Star Line, a shipping company. Your main rival, Cunard, has just launched the passenger liner *Lusitania*. At 790 feet (241 meters) long, she is huge and very fast. At a London dinner party with William Pirrie, you discuss the highly lucrative sea route between Europe and the United States. Lord Pirrie is a director of Harland and Wolff, the Belfast-based shipbuilders who have built all of White Star's vessels. You decide to think big and plan to build three ships that are heavier than the *Lusitania*'s 30,000 tons, and 100 feet (30 m) longer. With luxurious and speedy transatlantic crossings, you will attract the wealthy passenger trade and the growing number of emigrants traveling to North America.

On April 10, 1912, at 12:00 noon, the *Titanic* will leave Southampton, England, on her maiden voyage. The ship will set out to cross the Atlantic Ocean and plans to arrive in New York seven days later. She is the largest ship in the world and, for her wealthy first-class passengers, certainly the most luxurious. At this point, you definitely want to sail on the *Titanic*. Little do you know that the ship is sailing toward disaster...

Designing the *Titanic*

J. Bruce Ismay

I have a dream, to build three ships more luxurious than the world has ever seen.

The architects and draftsmen at the Harland and Wolff shipyard work hard to make the planned superliners a reality. While the plans for the ships are drawn up, three dry docks are converted into two—no existing dry dock is large enough to build the huge new liners! On July 29, 1908, the plans are ready. The keel plate for *Olympic*, the first of the three giant liners, is laid on December 16, 1908. The keel plate for the second liner is laid three months later, on March 31, 1909. Her name is *Titanic*.

You were born in Liverpool, England, in 1862. Your father founded the White Star Shipping Line in 1869. In 1902, the White Star Line was sold to American financier J. P. Morgan, but you stayed on as managing director.

Although *Olympic* and *Titanic* are almost identical in size, *Titanic* is actually 1,004 tons heavier than her sister ship.

The third ship, *Gigantic*, is later renamed *Britannic*.

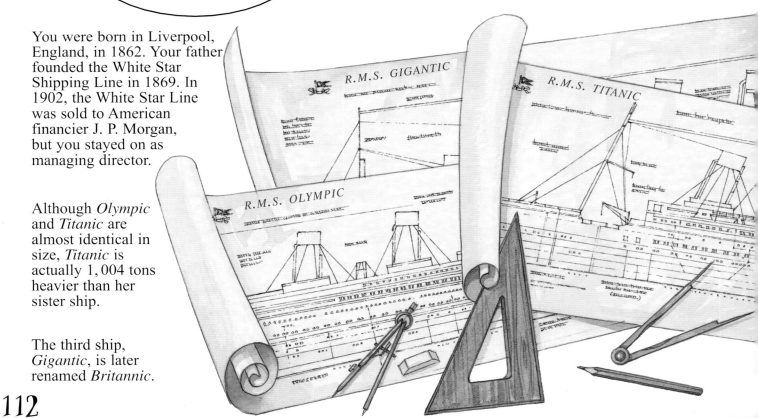

R.M.S. GIGANTIC

R.M.S. TITANIC

R.M.S. OLYMPIC

Building the "Unsinkable" Ship

You have the plans, you have the dry dock, and now you need workers. The shipyard employs approximately 11,300 men to build *Titanic*. The central girders are first riveted to the keel to make the spine of the hull. Then 350 steel frames, with 10 levels of deck supports, form the skeleton of the ship. Bulkheads divide *Titanic*'s hull into 16 compartments, which are said to be watertight because each extends well above the waterline. The ship could still float even if four of the compartments were filled with water! The shipyard is a dangerous place to work. Eight workers have been killed during construction, and over 240 accidents have been recorded by Harland and Wolff.

Aaah!

RIVETERS. They rivet steel plates, up to 6 feet (2 m) high and 36 feet (11 m) wide, weighing 5 tons, to the frames.

ANCHORS. *Titanic* needs three anchors. The heaviest weighs over 17 tons and will need a team of 20 horses to pull it from the foundry to the shipyard.

Launched but Not Completed

O n May 31, 1911, *Titanic*'s empty hull slides down the slipway. Sixty-two seconds later she enters the water for the first time. According to the custom of the shipyard and the White Star Line, the ship is launched unchristened.

Launch
OF
White Star Royal Mail
Triple-Screw Steamer
"TITANIC"

At Belfast,
Wednesday, 31st May, 1911, at 12.15 p.m.
Admit Bearer

Launch invitation

Who's Who?

Chief engineer   **Electrician**   **Boiler-maker**

Fireman   **Stoker**   **Trimmer**

Greaser   **Apprentice**

BOILER ROOMS. Seventy-three trimmers (who break up coal into small lumps) and 177 firemen work in the boiler rooms.

There are 29 boilers on this ship!

Yes, each 16 feet 6 inches (5 m) high!

DOWN THE SLIPWAY. To get the massive ship down to the water, over 23 tons of soap, grease, and train oil are used. *Titanic* slides almost 1,800 feet before being brought to a halt by six anchor chains and two other piles of chains weighing 80 tons each.

Handy Hint

Yaaawwn

If you want a job as a stoker, wait at the dock just before the ship sets sail. Casual labor is hired at the last minute as replacements for any crew members who fail to turn up.

Bloomin' backbreaking work for $27 a month.

All the machinery, including the engines, boilers, and funnels, is installed on board once the ship is afloat by using floating cranes. Once this is completed, the vessel can be towed away to a fitting-out berth. *Titanic*'s interior will take 10 months and several million man-hours to complete. On April 2, 1912, the completed *Titanic* sets sail to begin its sea trials.

117

Captain and Crew

Captain Edward John Smith has been commodore of the White Star fleet since 1904. As he usually commands the White Star's newest ship, he will take charge of *Titanic* on her maiden voyage. Captain Smith is popular with his passengers and crew. Some wealthy passengers refuse to sail across the Atlantic unless he is captain. His salary is twice as much as a Cunard captain's, at $6,250 a year (that equals about $73,000 today), plus a no-collision bonus of $200! It will be Smith's last voyage, as he is retiring.

Members of the Crew

CAPTAIN SMITH. He is in charge of 892 crew members, divided into three departments. The deck department is made up of 73 officers and seamen. The engine department has 325 crew, and the steward department has 494.

Captain

OFFICERS. The officers are paid between $45 and $125 per month depending on length of service and experience.

Officer

SEAMEN. The able seamen are paid about $25 per month, depending on their duties. The deck crew works shifts of four hours on and eight hours off.

Seaman

If only we could get to New York in time to make the morning papers!

We don't want to force the engines when we are breaking them in, Mr. Ismay.

Handy Hint
(for crew only)

Sluurrp

Be very nice to the passengers— tips can really boost your pay.

The Power of Steam

TRIPLE-SCREW STEAMER. *Titanic* is a triple-screw (three-propeller) steamer with five engines. Steam is produced in the six boiler rooms and piped to the engine rooms. Once the steam has passed through the engines, it is piped to the condensers, where it is cooled back into water and reused.

STEWARDS AND STEWARDESSES. Their duties and pay depend on which part of the ship they work in. Some wait on tables, others attend to cabins. One stewardess's monthly pay is about $17 for working 17 hours a day.

Stewardess and steward

Chef

CHEFS. There are two onboard chefs who supervise the two kitchens and a total of 35 cooks.

STOREKEEPERS. There are two storekeepers with two assistants on board.

Storekeeper

All Aboard

Now the crew can welcome passengers aboard. There are three categories of passengers: first class, second class, and steerage (third class). You will travel in first class, naturally.

Manservant Lady's maid Nanny

•R.M.S. TITANIC•
FIRST CLASS PASSAGE
TO NEW YORK
2 ADULTS
1 CHILD
3 SERVANTS
$750

•R.M.S. TITANIC•
SECOND CLASS PASSAGE
TO NEW YORK
2 ADULTS
1 CHILD
$145

First-class passengers travel in the most comfortable areas of the ship—the luxurious accommodation will attract the wealthy. Steerage passengers stay in the lower, less desirable parts of the ship. Many of these poorer passengers are emigrating to North America, looking for a new life.

STEERAGE. The accommodation in the steerage section of the ship is basic compared to other sections of the liner. Single men and women in steerage are separated by the entire length of the ship—men in the bow, women in the stern. Families are housed together in cabins.

•R.M.S. TITANIC•
THIRD CLASS PASSAGE
TO NEW YORK
2 ADULTS
2 CHILDREN
$120

Handy Hint
(for millionaires only)

Try to reserve a parlor suite with a 50-foot (15-m)-long private promenade deck. Book early to avoid disappointment—there are only two, and they cost $4,350 each (this would be about $70,000 today!).

Other Travelers

There will be plenty of dogs on *Titanic*, so an informal dog show is being planned for Monday, April 15.

Stocking the Ship
What You Will Need for a Transatlantic Crossing:

Titanic's food stores and equipment included:

11,000 pounds of fresh fish
4,000 pounds of dried fish
7,500 pounds of bacon and ham
25,000 pounds of poultry and game
2,500 pounds of sausages
1,500 gallons of fresh milk
44,000 pieces of cutlery
29,000 items of glassware
75,000 pounds of fresh meat
40,000 fresh eggs
40 tons of potatoes
800 bundles of asparagus
1,000 bottles of wine
15,000 bottles of ale and stout
12,000 dinner plates
1,000 oyster forks
15,000 champagne glasses
40,000 towels
45,000 table napkins
5 grand pianos
14 wooden lifeboats
2 wood cutters,
3,560 life jackets
49 life buoys
4 Englehardt collapsible boats—total lifeboat capacity 1,178 (Hold on, there are 2,206 passengers and crew! Never mind, the ship is "unsinkable" after all...)

The ship's full name is R.M.S. *Titanic* — the R.M.S. stands for Royal Mail Ship, as she will be used for shipping mail between Britain and the United States. There is a rumor that gold bars are also on board—but gold is transported and recorded as "mail" to keep it secret. *Titanic's* huge hold is filled with all sorts of things, from walnuts to ostrich feathers. Some of the wealthy passengers are even taking cars with them.

Five grand pianos?!

Don't worry, we'll squeeze 'em all in.

Handy Hint

Make sure all your items are insured. The total worth of the cargo on board *Titanic* in 1912 is $420,000, or about $6.7 million today.

Watch Out! Leaving Southampton

Rich and Famous On Board

John Jacob Astor VI

Benjamin Guggenheim

Mr. & Mrs. Isidor Straus

Colonel Archibald Gracie

At noon on April 10, 1912, *Titanic* sets off from Southampton. Swift action by Captain Smith avoids a collision with another ship docked there, the *New York*. *Titanic* reaches Cherbourg, France, at dusk, where the wealthiest of the passengers embark. On April 11, *Titanic* arrives in Queenstown, Ireland, before setting off across the Atlantic.

MONEY, MONEY, MONEY. Among the first-class passengers is John Jacob Astor VI, the richest man on board. Benjamin Guggenheim's family made a fortune from mining, and Isidor Straus is the founder of Macy's department store in New York. Colonel Gracie's account of *Titanic*'s maiden voyage will make him famous one day.

Route to New York

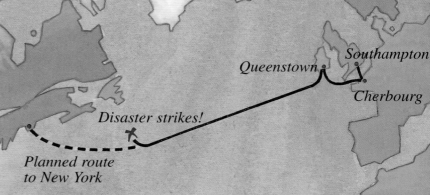

Southampton

Queenstown

Cherbourg

Disaster strikes!

Planned route to New York

Handy Hint

Ignore the 1898 book *Futility*. It tells the tale of a ship sinking on its maiden voyage with many lives lost due to too few lifeboats.

Oooh!

The wash from *Titanic*'s huge propellers causes the *New York* to break her moorings and pulls her straight into the path of the *Titanic* (below).

Aaaargh!

A Tour of the Ship

FIRST-CLASS STATEROOMS. Working fireplaces are just one of the features in these lavishly decorated rooms. The rooms can accommodate one, two, or three people.

Some of these First-class cabins have to share a bathroom!

Your designers and shipbuilders have done a wonderful job, especially with the first-class sections. The dining rooms are elegant and spacious, and there are luxurious staterooms, cafés, and libraries. The main forward staircase is one of the ship's most dramatic features, lit from above by natural

First Class

STEERAGE. Third-class passengers stay in four-berth cabins. These are rather comfortable and would be used in second class on other ships.

There are only 2 bathtubs for the 710 passengers in third class!

Drone, drone, drone…

126

light through a huge domed skylight. *Titanic* has three elevators in the first-class section and is the first ship to have one for second-class passengers. She is also the first ocean liner to have a swimming pool and a gym. Although second-class cabins are bigger and more luxurious than those in steerage, they look small and bare compared to the sumptuous rooms on the higher decks.

Handy Hint

Wheeze!

Try out the exercise machines in the gymnasium in first class. Passengers traveling in second class are allowed to look around first class before the ship sets sail.

Second Class

Steerage (Third Class)

Icebergs Ahead....

Captain's Log: April 14, 1912

...the engines have never run so fast...

Captain Smith is a guest of Mr. and Mrs. Widener at dinner in the restaurant on B deck.

Another warning, Captain.

He receives another message about icebergs—the sixth warning today.

The ship is now steaming toward New York at speeds of more than 22.5 knots (26 mph)—so fast that she will arrive a day early. Ice warnings are coming in from other ships in this area of the North Atlantic. The lookout crew in the crow's nest have been warned to watch out for icebergs—but their binoculars were left behind in Southampton! At 11:40 P.M., you are awoken by strange scraping noises. Putting a coat on over your pajamas, you head for the ship's bridge. Captain Smith tells you the ship has struck ice and is seriously damaged, but you don't believe him.

It's very cold, Officer Lightoller.

One degree above freezing, sir.

It is a moonless evening, and the sea is calm. Captain Smith leaves the bridge to go to bed at 9:20 P.M.

When the watch changes at 10:00 P.M., Officer Murdoch takes charge of the wheel on the bridge.

11:40 P.M. Lookouts spot an iceberg. The ship's engines are put into reverse, but it is too late, and *Titanic* scrapes along the side.

Crrrunch!

Handy Hint

Send emergency messages by Morse code. Use the traditional distress signal, CQD, and try the new one, SOS, because it is quicker and easier to send.

DAMAGE TO THE SHIP. Hitting the iceberg made the hull plates buckle. The water pressure on the weakened joints makes the rivets pop out, and the plates are pushed apart.

We've struck an iceberg, sir!

11:50 P.M. Captain Smith returns to the bridge and orders the watertight doors closed. This will make the ship unsinkable.

MIDNIGHT. You both inspect the ship. Water is gushing into the hull, flowing above the bulkheads and pulling the ship down.

Captain Smith faces the grim reality that his ship is sinking. The telegraph operator begins sending emergency messages.

129

Wake Up! Life Jackets On!

What Do You Do?

PANIC?!

Stay calm...

...or stay in bed?!

Soon after midnight, Captain Smith orders the lifeboats prepared, and adds that women and children should evacuate *Titanic* before the men. The first lifeboat, number seven, splashes into the water at 12:25 A.M., 45 minutes after the collision. It contains 28 passengers, but has space for 65. By 1:20 A.M., six lifeboats have left the ship. Deep in the boiler and engine rooms, engineers and crew risk their own safety to keep the lights burning and the pumps working. You help people into the lifeboats, then quietly slip yourself into collapsible boat C.

COME BACK! Using a megaphone, Captain Smith orders several of the half-empty lifeboats to return to the ship to pick up more passengers. None respond because they are afraid of becoming overloaded.

SINKING? I DON'T BELIEVE IT. Few passengers believe that the ship is really sinking. The thought of descending into the darkness of the icy Atlantic makes many people stay on deck in the hope of being rescued. A lot of the female passengers refuse to be separated from their husbands.

Sinking Fast

How *Titanic* Sinks

BULKHEADS. Six compartments are split open, and even the watertight doors cannot save the ship.

FRONT FIRST. The weight of the water in the front compartments pulls the bow of the ship downward.

BOW SUBMERGED. The ship tears apart, and the bow heads for the ocean floor.

FINAL MINUTES. The stern bobs upright for five minutes before filling with water and sinking.

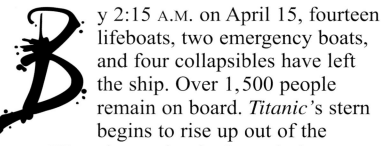

y 2:15 A.M. on April 15, fourteen lifeboats, two emergency boats, and four collapsibles have left the ship. Over 1,500 people remain on board. *Titanic*'s stern begins to rise up out of the ocean. Water is pouring in through the open portholes. The ship's lights are still on, and the band bravely continues to play on deck. At 2:18 A.M., the lights start to flicker off and on. Rivets begin to pop, and deck planks snap as the ship begins to break in two. The noise is deafening. Once the bow is totally submerged, it finally rips apart from the rest of the ship and plunges to the ocean floor. Just a few minutes later, you turn your back as *Titanic*'s stern slides under the water. Captain Smith is last seen on the bridge, having given final orders to abandon ship.

Handy Hint

Help the crew of your lifeboat row away from the ship so you aren't sucked down with her when she sinks.

Molly Brown

Mrs. Margaret Brown becomes known as the "Unsinkable Molly Brown" for taking command of lifeboat number 6 and demanding that women be allowed to row as well as men.

TITANIC

133

The Aftermath

Only one person is rescued alive from the freezing sea. Over 1,500 lives are lost, but only 306 of those bodies are picked up. The dead from first class are embalmed and taken home for burial, but those from third class and crew members are sewn up in heavy linen and buried at sea. The wages of the 214 surviving crew are calculated and paid up to the moment the ship sank.

At the official inquiries that follow, many questions are asked: Should *Titanic* have been sailing more slowly? Should she have carried more lifeboats? After the disaster, a change in the law ensures that all passenger ships carry enough lifeboats for everyone on board and that regular lifeboat drills be held. All ships also have to have 24-hour radio watch.

They are frozen to death, not drowned.

There's someone alive!

S.S. Carpathia to the Rescue

S.S. *CARPATHIA*. This Cunard ship is 58 miles (93 km) away from *Titanic* when she receives the SOS signal. She steams to the scene of the disaster and arrives at 4:10 A.M.

SURVIVORS TAKEN TO NEW YORK. *Carpathia* cruises the area looking for any last survivors before setting sail for New York with 705 of *Titanic*'s stunned passengers on board.

What Happens to You?

J. BRUCE ISMAY. What has happened to J. Bruce Ismay, the man who dreamed of building the greatest liners in the world? You have survived the disaster, but your reputation is ruined. Within a year you resign from the White Star Line and donate $50,000 to the pensions fund for widows of *Titanic* crew. You die in 1937 at the age of 74, having never made any further public statement about *Titanic* since the inquiries into the disaster.

Glossary

Armada The Spanish word for a fleet.

Baleen Plates that grow in the mouths of some whales. They filter the krill and small fish that whales feed on.

Beacon A large fire that can be seen from a distance and acts as a signal.

Berth A fixed bunk on a ship for sleeping in, or a ship's place in dock.

Bible leaves A lump of whale blubber, sliced into sections that open out like the pages of a book.

Blanket piece A long strip of blubber cut from the body of a whale.

Blubber A layer of fat that protects animals such as whales and seals from cold weather.

Bow The front end of a boat or ship.

Bowsprit A small mast that projects from the front of a ship.

Breech The bottom part of a gun barrel, where the cannonball (or bullet) lies before the gun is fired.

Bridge The control room on a ship.

Bulkhead An upright partition separating the compartments of a ship.

Cannon A large gun on wheels.

Church of England The English branch of the Christian Church, with the British monarch at its head.

Civil rights Personal and property rights that are legal and recognized by the government.

Collapsible boat A type of lifeboat that is folded up for storage.

Colony A distant territory settled by emigrants, which is under the control of their home country.

Commodore The senior captain of a shipping line.

Congregation A group of people who gather together for religious worship.

Contingent A group of people who represent an area or a larger group.

Cooper A craftsman who makes and repairs wooden barrels.

CQD The standard ship distress call, first used in 1903. "CQ" was the signal for listening radio operators to stop and pay attention; adding the "D" meant "distress."

Crow's nest A lookout platform high up on the mast of a ship.

Culverin A powerful type of cannon with a long barrel.

Cutting stage A wooden platform on the side of a whaling ship.

Democracy A government elected by the people.

Descendant A person whose history can be traced to a particular individual or family.

Dry dock An area for building or repairing ships, from which water can be pumped out.

Emigrate To leave one country to settle in another.

Evict To force someone to leave their home, legally or illegally.

Fever Any kind of illness in which a high temperature is one of the symptoms.

Fireship A ship deliberately set on fire and sent toward an enemy ship.

First mate The second-in-command on a merchant ship.

Flensing The process of stripping the blubber and other valuable parts from a whale.

Flintlock musket An early form of a gun.

Galleass A large ship powered by oars and sails and used to transport troops.

Galleon A large, slow-moving, and heavily armed ship.

Galley A large ship powered by oars and sails. It was heavily armed and was used to transport troops and attack enemy ships and towns.

Gombeen man An Irish term for a moneylender or shopkeeper who sells goods to poor people on credit and charges a high rate of interest.

Gunpowder Explosive black powder.

Hardtack A kind of hard, saltless biscuit eaten at sea.

Harpoon A type of spear that is used for catching whales and large fish.

Horse pieces Sections of blubber.

Hull The body or frame of a ship.

Keel The "backbone" of a ship along which the rest of the hull is built up.

Kerosene Liquid fuel.

Krill Small sea creatures eaten by whales.

Lay Wages for the crew of a whaling ship—a share of the earnings of a voyage.

Legacy Something that is handed down from an ancestor.

Marrow The fatty substance found inside bones.

Match In the 16th century, a piece of burning rope used to fire a cannon.

Mooring A fixed object that a ship can be tied to.

Morale The level of confidence of a person or group of people.

Morse code A set of dots, dashes, and spaces used to send messages via radio to other ships or to land.

Musket A long-barreled gun that fired a ball of lead.

Muzzle The open end of a gun.

Nantucket sleigh ride When a boat is dragged along by a harpooned whale.

New World A term used to describe North and South America.

Oakum Hemp or jute fiber, usually mixed with tar, that was used to make wooden ships watertight.

Pilgrims The name first used by William Bradford to describe the group of Separatists who moved to Leiden. The term Pilgrims was used later to describe all of the Separatists who traveled to America aboard the *Mayflower*.

Pitch A dark, sticky substance like tar, used to seal the gaps between ships' timbers.

Plimoth Colony The settlement established by the Pilgrims in December 1620 at present-day Plymouth, Massachusetts.

Pod A family group of whales.

Poop house The living quarters of the captain on board ship, located at the stern and above the level of the main deck.

Pope The head of the Roman Catholic Church.

Porthole A window in the side of a ship.

Portuguese man-of-war A sea creature which resembles a jellyfish, but is really a group of separate animals living together. It has a very painful sting.

Privateer A person given permission by his government or ruler to raid enemy merchant ships.

Provisions Supplies for a journey.

Puritans The name given in the 16th century to the more extreme English Protestants who believed in strict religious discipline.

Quadrant An instrument used for taking measurements at sea to find a ship's position.

Quay (pronounced like "key") A platform next to the water where ships are loaded and unloaded.

Rigging The network of ropes used to support the masts and sails of a ship.

Rivet A metal pin for holding sheets of metal together.

Rudder The piece of machinery used for steering a ship.

Sailcloth Tough canvas used to make ships' sails.

Scrimshaw Intricate designs carved into whale teeth or bone.

Seaworthy Capable of sailing on open seas without undue risk of sinking.

Seed potatoes Potatoes that are not eaten, but saved and planted to grow the next year's crop.

Separatists Radicals who broke away from the Church of England during the reign of Queen Elizabeth I to establish their own independent congregations.

Shallop A small open boat, used primarily in shallow water.

Shipkeeper The person who looks after a whaling ship while the rest of the crew are away in the whaleboat.

Shot A missile fired from a cannon, such as a cannonball.

Shrouds Part of the rigging of a sailing ship: a series of ropes that help to brace the mast, with smaller ropes tied across them to make a sort of ladder for the crew.

Sliding coffin A coffin with a removable bottom, so that a body can be dropped from it into the grave, and the same coffin can then be used again for other bodies.

SOS The Morse code distress signal that came into official use in 1908.

Spade A sharp tool used for cutting blubber from a dead whale's body.

Spanish Netherlands An area of northern Europe controlled by Spain in the 16th century. It was made up of parts of present-day France, Belgium, and the Netherlands.

Spermaceti A waxy substance from the head of sperm whales.

Squadron A unit of warships.

Steerage An area in the middle of a ship where the crew normally slept.

Stern The back end of a boat or ship.

Steward A person on a ship who looks after the supplies.

Swab To wash thoroughly.

Touchhole The point on the outside of a gun barrel through which the charge of gunpowder inside is ignited.

Transatlantic Spanning across the Atlantic Ocean.

Treaty A formal agreement between two or more groups to establish terms of peace or trade.

Trying out Converting whale blubber into oil by boiling the blubber in a metal try pot.

Typhus An infectious disease that includes such symptoms as fever, weakness, and a skin rash.

Ventilation The forced movement of air around a room.

Wadding Any soft material used for packing.

Waterline The line along which the surface of water touches the side of a ship.

Whaleboat A small ship from which a whale is harpooned.

Whale oil Oil derived from the blubber and spermaceti of large whales.

Whipstaff A vertical wooden bar attached to a tiller, which in turn was attached to the rudder, to steer a ship.

Workhouse A place where poor people were housed and fed at public expense. In return, they were required to do simple physical work.

Wrecker A person who collects items from a shipwreck.

Note: Ireland, Britain, and England
During the period described in *You Wouldn't Want to Sail on an Irish Famine Ship*—in fact, from 1801 to 1922—Ireland, England, Scotland, and Wales were all part of the United Kingdom of Great Britain and Ireland. The whole kingdom was ruled by the British government in London, England. But the English had been fighting over Ireland since the Middle Ages—long before Great Britain was formed in 1707. Most of the island of Ireland became a separate country in 1922 (it has been the Republic of Ireland since 1949), but today, Northern Ireland is still part of the United Kingdom.

Index